FIF

P. O. Box 772
DETROIT LAKES, MINN. 56501

THRILLING STORIES
OUT OF THE
SERVICEMEN'S CENTERS

by

DOROTHY MYERS

CENTER PRESS
RANTOUL, ILLINOIS

DEDICATED TO

The beloved Founder and Director of
Christian Service Centers, Inc.

REV. E. W. CROCKETT

Through whose ministry thousands have
found Christ precious, including me.

CONTENTS

CONTENTS

ABOUT THE AUTHOR

Thirty-six years ago the angels of God rejoiced over one soul that was saved,but because of this one, thousands have been brought to the Saviour from many parts of the world. Miss Dorothy Myers gave her heart and life to the Lord Jesus in our Center in Rantoul when she was a timid and reserved young lady in her early twenties. Immediately after her conversion God placed His hand upon her and gave her a heavy burden for the lost. Through tears of dedication her life was given over to be used of the Lord. God gave her a sincere hunger to know His Word. In the first year she was saved, she read her Bible through five times and memorized hundreds of Bible Verses.

One day I asked her, "What would you rather do more than anything else in the world?" The answer to this question came without hesitation, "I would rather be a soul-winner for Jesus than anything else in all the world."

This resolution marked the beginning of Dorothy Myers'

ministry with the Christian Service Centers, which was to touch the lives of thousands of young men and women in military service from all over the world. World War II was in its early stages and thousands of America's finest young men were leaving Chanute Field for the battlefields, many of them never to return. Along with these from our own country, choice young men from many other Nations were sent to Chanute Field for training. In answer to much prayer, the Holy Spirit directed them into the Servicemen's Center where they could hear the gospel and be saved.

Dorothy had a rugged home life on the family farm (near Chanute Field). Although yet unsaved, her parents had high moral standards for their children. They were taught to obey, work and endure hardness. In those depression days there was a struggle for survival. She often tells of treading through muddy roads, as a little girl, three miles to school, carrying her meager lunch and books. However hard, this built a strong body and developed the integrity that must characterize her life for the years ahead. God makes no mistakes.

Although by nature she was a timid and reserved girl, from that first dedication God began to use her in unusual ways. Volumes could be written about her experiences of precious souls coming to the Saviour. These include officers, enlisted young men and women, and young officers from many other nations, while here for training, who would come into the Center and receive the Lord Jesus Christ as their Saviour. Recently a Lt. Commander came in to see me at the San Antonio Center and told me how Dorothy helped him in a great crisis time in his life. Old people, little children, salesmen, grocery men, and many many more outside the military have been saved through her faithfulness. On the train, on the bus and in planes, people have been saved through her witness. Pastors, missionaries and Christian business men over the world are some of the results of her love and testimony for the Lord Jesus. The stories in this little booklet are just a few of the thousands of experiences she has had in reaching the lost.

On one occasion, during the Korean War days, I asked her to take charge of our newly established Center in San Antonio, Texas, while I was having revival meetings in Eastern Canada. During those six weeks she had two hundred and ninety three to bow the knee and call upon the Lord Jesus Christ to save them. Young men were going to fight and die. They wanted to know the way to Heaven.

Day by day, putting in long hours, Miss Dorothy, as she is often endearingly called by the servicemen, still pleads with the unsaved to come to Christ. Those of us who have worked beside her are still amazed at the way God uses her. She has sacrificed many things because of her love for Christ and the souls of men. She could have had a home, family, a car, and many of the comforts of life, but she chose rather to live on a meager income, —then sacrificing even more to put back all she could into the ministry she loved. Her private quarters consist of a limited space provided by the Center. Her "home" has always been the Service Center where she has made a "home-away-from-home" for thousands of servicemen. Our official Board love her enough that they would have provided anything she wanted. Her sincerest desires are not for material things, but rather to please the Lord Jesus, who said, ". . .foxes have holes, and the birds of the air have nests; but the Son of man hath not where to lay His head."

Miss Dorothy could be weary and worn, or sick, but she never lost an opportunity to touch a life with the glorious gospel of Jesus Christ. Thousands will rise up in glory and call her blessed because she was faithful to show them the Way.

". . . .he that winneth souls is wise." —Prov. 11:30 "And they that be wise shall shine as the brightness of the firmament; and they that turn many to righteousness as the stars for ever and ever." —Daniel 12:3

E. W. Crockett, Exec. Dir.

CHRISTIAN SERVICE CENTERS, Inc.

(A brief historical sketch)

Some years ago I wrote this article for our Good News Bulletin. I believe it will give the proper setting and a brief history of our ministry that you may better appreciate the great work of God with our military young people.

"Call unto Me and I will answer thee and show thee great and mighty things which thou knowest not."
—Jeremiah 33:3

At the beginning of 1941, war for our nation was very evident, and preparation became more intense day by day. Chanute Field, near Rantoul, Illinois, began to boom in the building and expansion, and thousands of American youth were called in for training.

With the impending tragedies of war ahead, a merciful God, knowing that men would die by the thousands, and *"not willing that any should perish,"* was moving hearts to meet the desperate spiritual needs. The servant He chose for this unprecedented ministry for this crucial hour was E. W. Crockett, a young pastor in a town forty miles from Rantoul. Compelled by the Spirit of the living God, his feet firmly planted on Jer. 33:3, Brother Crockett *"launched out into the deep."*

As *"by faith, Noah, being warned of God of things not seen as yet, moved with fear, prepared an ark. . . .",* so the same God was moving another man to action. By faith Mr. Crockett leased a piece of ground in Rantoul and began a building, —the first Servicemen's Center in existence. While most Christians were unmindful of what God was doing in their midst, this man toiled on, much of the time alone, through the days and long into the nights.

When Pearl Harbor fused the fire in every American, our Service Center ministry was well underway. Lonesome servicemen, knowing the battlefields were just a few weeks ahead, roamed the streets with heavy hearts. During those war years, the Center doors were never closed, day nor night. While others slept the Center workers labored on, winning precious souls to Christ. As always, bearing the heaviest load was our Director, laboring long hours, often without time for sleep nor food. God gave the promised strength. Thousands of boys were saved as they knelt in the prayer room and went out to face the battle with Christ in their hearts.

Honoring the faith of His servant as he claimed Jer. 33:3, God moved mountains and wrought mighty miracles. Thousands of dollars had been spent and God had supplied every need.

In 1944, Brother Crockett launched out again. Inside of a few weeks another Center in Gulfport, Mississippi was beaming forth the gospel message, in spite of all the impossibilities and can'ts of man. Jer. 33:3 was proven again!

The mercy of God is greater than human conception and in 1945, God moved upon our Director's heart once more. This time we saw the foot-prints of God as a building was secured in Sioux Falls, South Dakota. Thousands of precious boys found Christ in this Center before they went to face the battle. (After World War II, the camps at Gulfport and Sioux Falls closed and eventually these two Centers.)

11

When the Korean War threatened in 1951, another great step of faith was taken, this time to establish a Center in San Antonio, Texas, near the famed Alamo. The Center, in the heart of this great city of a half million people, surrounded by six large military bases, has been used of God to reach literally thousands of young men for the Lord Jesus Christ.

When God's urgent call came again in 1957, arming himself again with Jer. 33:3, Brother Crockett set forth . . . this time to Norfolk, Virginia. Today, to the glory of God, a lovely Center flourishes here, in the midst of the largest Naval Center of the world. Thousands of sailor boys in glistening white uniforms throng the streets. This vast field, *"white unto harvest"* is being reaped.

"Come over and help us. . . ." This call in 1959 took this man of faith to Lawton, Oklahoma where another lighthouse for God began to shine forth the good news that Jesus saves.

Behind every great movement, God has a man, and we who serve in the Service Center ministry give praise to our God for the leader He has given us. We have found Mr. Crockett to be a man of great stability, yet one who, when the clear call of God is heard, is never afraid to move out by faith alone and possess the promised land. What a challenge to each of us!

We, who have worked with him for years, know him best. We are eye-witnesses to his sacrificial life, his great faith, his burning zeal and love for precious souls, and his untiring efforts as he has labored almost day and night in the work of the Lord. Yes, *"laboring more diligently than we all,"* yet somehow always having time to share and bear the joys and sorrows of each individual Center missionary, or others who have need . . . often at great cost to himself. We are indeed grateful for his unselfish love and personal concern, so often expressed in deeds of kindness.

It was for this reason, as an expression of our love and appreciation, that the Center missionaries, Board members, and loving friends presented Brother Crockett with an expense paid trip around the world. This trip was a missionary journey to seventeen different countries, visiting and encouraging many of our foreign servicemen who had been saved in our Centers, while they had been in America for training. (In Formosa alone there are hundreds of high ranking officers who have found Christ in our Centers.) Lack of space makes only a very brief account of this profitable trip possible, but everywhere Mr. Crockett went he was joyously and royally received and entertained by grateful men who were thankful for his ministry which had brought them to Christ.

It was many years ago when I first met Brother Crockett. Sitting under his ministry, I was greatly convicted of my lost condition and was graciously saved by the Christ he preached. Only a short time later, as he challenged young people with the cry of God's heart to reach a world lost and dying without Christ, God laid His hand upon me and I could only answer, "Here am I Lord, send me." I, along with countless thousands, shall be eternally grateful for this servant God has so mightily used.

Reprinted from
May 1956
POWER MAGAZINE
by Ted Miller

power

SERVICEMEN'S CENTER

MISS MYERS
reports for DUTY

Miss Myers Reports for Duty
by Ted Miller

The little town of Rantoul, Ill., was far from the battlefields during World War II, but its citizens were painfully close to heartbreak.

Day after day, townspeople saw empty trains roll into the station, swallow up hundreds of freshly trained airmen from nearby Chanute Field, and glide away from weeping wives and mothers to battle posts from which many would not return. Other trains brought in new recruits, and the procession of sorrow rolled on.

Dorothy Myers, a medium-sized brunette in her mid-20s, watched the sad scenes with a heavy heart. If there were only something she could do! There was, and she took a job at the Christian Servicemen's Center across the street from the train station. From that day on in March 1944, she could be seen at almost any hour of the day or night serving coffee and cookies to the servicemen who crowded the Center for free refreshments and relaxation.

But there was more at the Center than food and games. Whenever Miss Myers could slip away from the serving counter, she would begin a quiet and earnest conversation with a group of airmen. More often than not, one or several would soon follow her to a prayer room, where they knelt and sent up fervent prayers. Tears trickled down softened faces as men prayed to get right with God.

Over and over that scene recurred in following months as Miss Myers tirelessly served her country and her Saviour.

Though not in uniform, Dorothy Myers had "enlisted for the duration"—plus.

During the war years, Miss Myers labored long hours at the post God had assigned her. In one day alone she prayed with 32 servicemen who confessed Christ as Saviour.

Today, 12 years later, she's still at her place in the Servicemen's Center at Rantoul, and still winning recruits to God's army from among the 20,000 airmen stationed at famed Chanute Field.

The Center, located in down-town, Rantoul, is not pretentious in appearance. Its brick and window front differ little from the one-story shops flanking its sides, except that its neon signs and the lettering on the green awning offer free service to its customers.

Inside, the long, narrow room is neat and comfortable with upholstered chairs, writing desks, game tables and library. At the back is a kitchen, visible through a large serving window which often frames the smiling face of Miss Myers.

The friendly, wide smile and a sincere gaze are the first things you notice about Miss Myers. That, and a quiet manner that borders on shyness. In fact, she was once so shy, she says, that she could hardly speak to strangers. Then God moved powerfully upon her heart, and her one aim became to speak to strangers about their souls.

Often the conversation starts at the serving counter, where Miss Myers and a helper are serving cookies and coffee. When everyone is served, she usually asks if the boys are Christians and then gives her testimony of how much Christ means to her.

One fellow, Don, answered her question with: "I'm a baptized Christian, but not a saved one." She found he had been reading their Gospel tracts and was under conviction for his sin. But when she urged him to make a decision, Don said he'd think it over and come back later.

You probably won't come back," she answered, "but I'll be praying for you."

The airman left, but in a few minutes he returned to retrieve his forgotten hat. He saw Miss Myers kneeling beside a couch, praying, and her concern spoke to his heart. He stayed, and gave his heart to Christ. He later told her he had been an evil sinner and had been thinking of committing suicide. One year after his conversion, he had led 12 others to his Saviour while stationed in Germany.

Once an airman guard and his prisoner, passing through Rantoul, came into the Center for refreshments. Miss Myers witnessed to both of them, and the prisoner indicated he wanted to trust Christ as his Saviour. The guard, under strict orders, would not remove the handcuffs binding him to his prisoner nor would he go into the prayer room. So they prayed openly in the recreation room.

Afterward, Miss Myers told the guard, "You are free and he is bound, but in God's sight, you are actually bound in sin and he is free."

Freedom through Christ also came to a number of foreign airmen training at Chanute. When 200 Chinese fliers studied at Chanute during the war, some of them visited the Center and a Captain Chi was the first one converted.

The next night, Capt. Chi brought in ten officer friends. He talked to them in Chinese in the prayer room for a long time, then asked Miss Myers to come in and "talk serious" to them. After several hours of Bible research, five of them said they wanted to become real Christians.

One of these was a Major Chang, commander of the Chinese trainees at Chanute. Afterward, Major Chang said, "My rank means nothing to me now. I want to do this kind of work for my people." Every time he came to the Center after that, he brought two different Chinese officers with him and asked Miss Myers to tell them how to be saved. About 50 of them accepted Christ before the unit went back to China.

Other servicemen from South America, England, Greece and France were also saved at the Center.

Salvation and witnessing mean so much to Dorothy Myers because of her own experience with God. She was working on the airbase when an airman and his wife invited her to services at a church on the outskirts of town. She went, and heard the Gospel simply and powerfully preached by the pastor, the Rev. E. W. Crockett.

A church member, she realized she did not possess Christ's life, and she opened her heart to Him. Under the pastor's urging, she pored over her Bible until she had memorized hundreds of verses and read through the Bible five times the first year.

A Christian friend soon invited her to the newly opened Servicemen's Center to help with the work. She gladly went, but came home miserable that night, knowing that she should have told the men they needed Christ and she had failed to speak to one of them. She was too shy.

That happened again and again. Then one evening, she was praying with her girl friend at her side for courage to witness. She told God she was willing, but she just couldn't do it. Suddenly she felt a loving arm on her shoulders, and she looked up toward her girl friend. But her companion was not touching her. Miss Myers believes God gave her the impression of His own arm around her, showing his love for mankind. From that time on, she never had difficulty witnessing about the love of Christ. "It is a real miracle to me," she says.

Shortly after that, Miss Myers left her airbase job for the small salary, long hours, and eternal rewards of the Center.

The Rev. Crockett, who led Miss Myers to Christ, was also the founder of the Service Center. He first came to the area in 1942 from a Baptist pastorate in Chatsworth, Ill., when he saw the great need for the Gospel among servicemen at Chanute Field.

He started a preaching center on the edge of town. Soon he saw that a location in town would reach many more, and the store opposite the train station was discovered vacant. They opened the doors to servicemen in February 1943, depending on a three-legged stove to cook the coffee and heat all the water.

Immediately servicemen got saved as they talked to the tireless, friendly, deadly-serious preacher. A lean man with thinning hair who once turned down a lucrative sales-instructor's job, the Rev. Crockett was not content with the success of one Center; he soon opened two others at Gulfport, Miss., and Sioux Fall, S. Dak., overcoming terrific obstacles.

The latter Centers closed after the war, but a new, large one was opened in San Antonio, Tex., in the midst of six military bases.

The Centers have been organized as the Christian Service Centers, Inc., with Christian businessmen serving on the board of directors. The work is supported by gifts of individuals and churches who know of the strong testimony. The indispensable cookies that are served to servicemen are baked, carefully packaged, and mailed by friends in many states.

When Mr. Crockett's travels between Centers, radio program in Minnesota, and occasional revival meetings filled his schedule, the founder and executive director of the Centers came to depend on Miss Myers to run the Rantoul work. He says he couldn't have put it in better hands.

She is in charge, starting at 9 in the morning and closing at 10:30 at night. Much of the time she works alone, other times with Christian servicemen or church friends; and an average of over 50 are led to Christ every month. She prayed with 14 the week prior to the interview for this article.

Asked how she witnesses, Miss Myers explained she often starts out in friendly conversation, then offers a Gospel tract, and asks if the serviceman is a Christian, if he really knows he's going to Heaven.

"Most servicemen lack that assurance, even though they believe themselves Christians," she said. Then she may tell what joy and assurance the Lord gave her when she asked Christ to forgive her sins and she trusted His promises in the Bible to save her.

Mr. Crockett interrupted to say that Miss Myers quotes Scripture after Scripture about sin, talking in a quiet voice, never arguing, and rarely pausing. "I've seen her talk to six fellows at a time until the tears started rolling down their cheeks. Her sincerity and love are plain to the boys."

One who knows Dorothy Myers would not be unduly amazed at the report that, during a six-week visit to the Texas Center, she prayed with 293 servicemen for salvation. "It was truly white unto harvest," she explains simply.

"We sin by not witnessing for Christ," Miss Myers declares. "To be effective, one must be willing to be used by the Holy Spirit, then He gives a burden for souls and brings conviction to the person dealt with."

After decisions are made, Miss Myers shows converts where to find Bible verses of assurance, the prayer life, confession of sin, the pure walk, and especially II Corinthians 5:17, *If any man be in Christ, he is a new creature: old things are passed away; behold, all things are become new.*

They get a New Testament, a memory verse packet, and Miss Myers hopes they'll soon be winning others.

One serviceman, Jack Dieken, began kneeling to pray in the barracks at night after Miss Myers suggested it. A newcomer, David Heisey, laughed and swore at Jack, trying to make him angry. But Jack handed him a tract and said, "I am praying for you."

David finally went to church and to the Center with Jack, where he was saved. "For the first time in my life, I knew where I was going," David said. Twelve other barracks mates were saved through Jack's new testimony. David went on to win other servicemen in Europe.

"I'd rather do soul-winning than anything else, though it's as exhausting as scrubbing floors," says Miss Myers. And today there are servicemen in every corner of the globe, and wives of servicemen, who are thankful she didn't do anything else but win souls for God.

THE STORY OF MY CONVERSION

GOD DID A WONDERFUL THING
FOR ME

*"He brought me up out of an horrible pit, out of the miry clay,
and set my feet upon a rock, and established my goings. And
He hath put a new song in my mouth, even praise unto our
God: many shall see it, and fear, and shall trust in the Lord."*
— *Psalm 40:2, 3*

In a few days I shall celebrate my spiritual birthday, —
February 2, 1943. Once again I stand in awe at God's love
and mercy, as in memory I look *"back to the hole of the pit,
whence I was digged."* I lived for twenty-one years before
anyone cared enough for my soul to tell me how I could be
saved. I was known as a "good girl." I never smoked, drank
or did many other things that other young people did. I was a
member of the Methodist Church, taught Sunday School,
was very religious, ——but I was lost.

After graduation from High School, I secured a job at
Chanute Air Force Base near my hometown. Here I met a
serviceman and his wife, Mr. and Mrs. Gaylord Chizum, who
were born-again Christians, but for a long time I did not
know this because they did not tell me; neither did they
speak to me about my soul. One day they visited the
Servicemen's Center and after a challenge from Rev.
Crockett to yield their lives completely, they knelt at the feet
of Jesus. Something happened! The next time they met me,
Mrs. Chizum asked, "You are saved, aren't you, Dorothy?" I
had never before heard anything about being *"saved."*
Embarrassed and shocked, I could only honestly stammer,
"Well, I hope so." Not knowing how to continue witnessing,
she said nothing more to me, but how I thank God *"she did*

what she could." God used her few simple words and later, in my room, under great conviction, I searched the Bible trying to find the way to Heaven, but my eyes were blinded to God's truth by Satan, the god of this world.

One night these friends invited me to go with them to a Bible Study in the Service Center and I went. The message I do not remember, but during the invitation hymn, Rev. Crockett quoted Philippians 3:9 and made a few comments: *"And be found in Him, not having mine own righteousness, which is of the law, but that which is through the faith of Christ, the righteousness which is of God by faith:"* As he pled for souls, God opened the eyes of my understanding, showing me I could not save myself by my good works. I, Dorothy Myers, was a lost, hell-bound sinner and only Christ and His shed blood could save my soul. That night the Spirit of God led me to take an open stand for Jesus. I knelt at His feet, a broken, lost sinner and invited Him into my heart to be my Saviour. Immediately I was a new creation! God gave me a *"peace that passeth all understanding."* I knew I was saved and that Heaven was my eternal home. Immediately my heart went out to my family, my class of Sunday School girls, my friends, knowing they were lost. I spent the night writing and rewriting a thirty-two page letter home to my family, pleading with them to be saved. Immediately I began to read the Word of God and pray for the lost.

I drank in the Word at every Bible Study in the Center, and in a few short weeks I was under tremendous conviction of sin, —the sin of silence. Many times I knelt beside my bed confessing this sin to God. Often I saw the boys leave the Center, get on a train headed for the battlefields, perhaps to die, but I could not tell them about Jesus. I was too timid, backward and shy. One night after a Bible Study in the Center, God broke my heart and I knelt sobbing before Him, confessing that, after all He had done for me, I was failing Him. I was not telling the lost the wonderful gospel message with which He had entrusted me. The overwhelming desire of my heart was that God might touch my lips with a coal off the altar that I might tell His message of salvation which I kept locked in my heart. As I knelt sobbing, God drew near and put His arm of love around me. It was so real that I looked up to see if I was mistaken and perhaps it was my girl-friend's arm. She did not have her arm around me. I have never attempted to explain what happened, only to say that God performed a miracle and fulfilled a promise in His Word. *"Delight thyself in the Lord, and He shall give thee the desires of thine heart."* The overwhelming desire of my heart was to be a soul-winner. That night God gave me that desire and loosed my tongue to proclaim His message to the lost. I, along with my Christian friends, was amazed that now I could easily and boldly approach the unsaved and plead with them to come to Christ and flee from the wrath to come.

Soon God gave me the joy of joys, —a soul for Jesus! I spent much time praying, handing out tracts, witnessing and leading the lost to Christ. That first year I read my Bible through five times and memorized hundreds of Bible verses. The Lord was so near and gracious, giving me the privilege of leading most of my family, my whole Sunday School class, and many of my friends to Jesus. Now, as I look back, I believe God was quickly preparing me for a greater service, —that of serving Him full-time in the Service Center. The need for laborers was urgent. Night and day, thousands of boys in uniform streamed in and out of Chanute Field, headed for the battle. Many would never return. Burdened with the tremendous need of reaching them for Christ, one day Rev. Crockett asked me, "Dorothy, what would you rather be more than anything else in the world?" Only one desire burned in my heart and I quickly answered, "More than anything else I want to be a soul-winner." Then he asked me to pray about working in the Center. God had already spoken to my heart about this and so only a year after I was saved, He led me into this wonderful ministry.

I stand in awe and amazement as I look back over these many years of service to the King of Kings and the Lord of

Lords. They have been glorious years and every step of the way I have felt His good hand upon me. Thousands upon thousands of times I have proclaimed His wonderful message of salvation, —but it never grows old or wearisome and each time I tell it I am again thrilled with the wonder of God's love. Thousands and thousands of times I have knelt in the presence of God with heartbroken sinners as they wept their way to the Saviour. We have wept and rejoiced with the angels and Jesus. Oh, the glory and magnitude of this holy calling!

As I step upon the threshold of another year in Jesus, my heart is full and God is near. Yet as I rejoice, a very solemn thought chills my heart and I share it with you. —What if Rev. Crockett had not obeyed God and started the Center here? —Had not challenged my friends to yield all to Christ? —Had not brought to me the message of salvation? Dear friends, not only would I be lost, but the thousands I have led to Christ would also spend eternity in Hell instead of Heaven. This tremendous responsibility which God has placed upon us who are saved should bring us to our knees.

Day after day as I stand witnessing for Christ, approximately 999 out of 1000 boys we speak to do not even KNOW the way to Heaven, —because no Christian cared enough to sit down with God's Word and show them. Somebody has failed them. Was it you? Can it be that your lips are sealed and somehow you cannot speak for Jesus? My friend, examine yourself. How long has it been since you wept for a soul? What is the *desire* of your heart? God shows no partiality; He only wants a channel through which He can give His Word. Will you be that channel? If you will, He will give you such abundant joy that you will taste of Heaven on earth. You will glorify Him by fulfilling His will, His purpose, the passion of His heart, —the salvation of souls. God help you to yield today.

> "Let me burn out for Thee, dear Lord
> Burn and wear out for Thee—

25

Don't let me rust, or my life be—
A failure my God to Thee—
Use me, and all that I have, dear Lord,
And get me so close to Thee
That I feel the throb of the great heart of God
And let me burn out for Thee."

Dear Reader,

In the thirty-six years I have served the Lord Jesus in the Christian Servicemen's Centers, the Lord has been pleased to let me kneel beside thousands of precious souls and lead them to a saving knowledge of the Lord Jesus Christ.

So, when I began the task of choosing some of those wonderful experiences to put in a book, I soon found myself overwhelmed with a host of thrilling experiences and many, many precious memories. I surely did not lack for material and so often Psalm 40:5 came to my heart in an anthem of praise to our wonderful God. "Many, O Lord my God, are thy wonderful

27

works which Thou hast done, and Thy thoughts which are to us-ward; they cannot be reckoned up in order unto Thee; if I would declare and speak of them, they are more than can be numbered."

In this preview booklet you will read a few of the stories which will be in a book that we are working on, which will be published, Lord willing, at a later date. We believe the time is short to serve Jesus, and we pray God will use this "short version" to bring glory to His Name and precious souls to the Saviour.

Most of these stories and articles were written as they happened, and were published from month to month in our Center publication, "The Good News Bulletin". As you read these every day accounts of God's mighty power in lives, my earnest prayer is that the Lord will draw near, — that you will completely yield your life to Jesus, — that you will feel the tug of God upon your heart, constraining you to be a witness to those 'round about who are yet lost and without the Saviour.

If this booklet is a blessing to you, may I suggest you order a goodly number and give them to your friends, — saved and unsaved. Perhaps you would like to read it in your family devotions. Give one to your pastor. Leave one in a nursing home. Pastor, give them to your members to encourage them in soul-winning. Perhaps as you read, God will reveal to you a particular person who will be blessed, or perhaps brought to the Saviour, by reading these pages.

Our only motive for writing this booklet is to glorify our great God and Saviour, Jesus Christ. All the labor of writing and publishing is lovingly and freely given to our precious Saviour who gave His all for us. Although it is not written for profit, if there is any, it will be used in the work so dear to our hearts, that of reaching our servicemen for Christ.

I would like to extend my grateful thanks to my many dear Christian friends who have been so faithful to support and pray for me and our ministry. My special love and thanks to my dear brother, Delmar, for his prayers, love and generous support these many years.

I am grateful for the many who have prayed and helped in the publishing of this booklet. Especially I thank Jon Kulison, a faithful, fellow-missionary, laboring in our Center at Norfolk, Virginia. Jon has spent many hours in prayer and labor in the preparing and printing of this booklet.

Above all, I thank my God for saving my sinful soul, and then calling me to the great privilege, but awesome responsibility, of serving Him.

"For we preach not ourselves, but Christ Jesus the Lord; and ourselves your servants for Jesus' sake. For God, who commanded the light to shine out of darkness, hath shined in our hearts, to give the light of the knowledge of the glory of God in the face of Jesus Christ. But we have this treasure in earthen vessels, that the excellency of the power may be of God, and not of us."

II Cor. 4:5-7

Dorothy Myers

A DAY IN
THE CHRISTIAN SERVICE CENTER

"...O Lord; in the morning will I direct my prayer unto thee, and will look up." —*Psalm 5:3*

"And my tongue shall speak of Thy righteousness and of Thy praise all the day long." —*Psalm 35:28*

Early mornings are usually quiet at the Center, so that is the time when we tidy up from the day before. You mothers know what a kitchen looks like after your sons have decided to get a lunch for themselves. Enough said!

As we finish cleaning, the 9:30 prayer hour has come, and all our workers gather in for a time of prayer. During this time we especially pray for precious souls: for our 'new born babes' and for our Christian boys, those here, and those who have gone from us.

Here come two servicemen to write letters. We invite them back to have a glass of lemonade. As we talk to them, we learn that they are waiting for a train to take them home on a three-day pass. Just a few hours at home, but they smile as they say, "It will be worth it, just to see Mother and Dad again." Then we give them a tract and inquire as to their soul's salvation, only to find that they know nothing about the gospel. The lemonade remains untouched as God speaks to the hearts of these two boys. The hands of one are shaking and a tear falls from the eyes of his buddy; and in response to my invitation to make this the day of salvation, one quickly responds, "Yes, Mam, I've always wanted to do what Jesus wanted me to, but I never understood it like this before." In our little prayer room these boys received the Lord Jesus, and the joy and peace that He alone can bring.

As the day goes on we talk to many—some who know they need Jesus, but are saying 'not today'—some not interested, some athiests. Oh, how these boys need our prayers.

It is six o'clock now, and here come our Christian boys, laughing and singing and rejoicing in the Lord. Sometimes they bring in a buddy for us to talk to, and many times that buddy is saved. They gather around the piano and sing, eat cookies, drink lemonade, or write letters. They even enjoy K.P. in our kitchen.

The witnessing for our Lord still goes on, and as we speak to two Chinese Officers, they say, "We not Christians yet." It is hard to make them understand, but after going over and over the plan of salvation in simple child-like language, they, too, give their hearts to the Lord.

As the night wears on, and others are dealt with, one more—a soldier, who comes in looking for a room for his wife, is saved. As I say good-bye to him, I see that it is twelve o'clock, and time to close a long happy day. The Christian fellows are in the prayer room praising God for his goodness, for the souls He gave us, and with burdened hearts ask Him to use them to win their friends to Christ. I slip in and on my knees breathe a prayer too.

"I will praise Thee forever, because Thou hast done it."
—Psalm 52:9

A HOME FOR VJELLMAR

This wonderful little story happened during World War II, and will be a blessing to many people. Vjellmar is a Norwegian boy who was sent to America for training. How grateful we are that God brought him into the Christian Service Center.

Vjellmar was a shy boy, but when we approached him about his soul, his face beamed and he said, "Yes, I want to go to Heaven someday to be with my mother." As we continued speaking to him, we realized he had never been born again, but was trusting in good works to take him to Heaven. God spoke to his heart through the precious Word of God, and Vjellmar wanted to receive the Lord Jesus Christ as his own personal Saviour. In the prayer room we knelt together and he called upon the Name of the Lord for salvation. Crying, because of his new-found joy, in broken English he said, "I don't like to cry before a lady, but I can't help it. I am so happy. God has saved my life many times, but this is the first time He has saved my soul."

That day we learned that Vjellmar's home was far north in Norway, so far north that they seldom ate anything but reindeer meat. A ship came in once each year with supplies. He told of going out to herd reindeer, taking along a piece of reindeer meat for lunch. By lunch time it would be so cold and frozen that he would have to put it in his glove to thaw it out before he could eat it.

When the Germans overtook Norway, Vjellmar was there. He tells that the English would drop radios for the Norwegian people to send messages back to them, telling how far the Germans were progressing and what they were doing. Vjellmar's father received one of the radios. One night at dusk, he went out to a lonely hill to send a message. As a cover-up he took his five year old son with him so the Germans would think they were just taking a walk. As they were sending the message to the English, the Germans caught them. The next day the Germans called out the whole village, and with Vjellmar, his mother, and sister in the front row, they shot his father and little five year old brother. They were told if anyone turned his head away, they, too, would be shot.

Then Vjellmar was taken away and put to work on an under-ground passage. While working there he learned that his mother and little sister had also been shot because they had not destroyed the Bible in their home. Vjellmar went back to the village and found that his loved ones had not even been buried. On Vjellmar's finger was a ring, battered and bent, which he took from his mother's finger before he buried her. She had been beaten so badly he could hardly recognize her. Some time later, when he was in England, he learned that the girl he had planned to marry had been taken by the Germans into Germany. Finally he received word she had died.

Vjellmar was left alone, heart-broken, and sad, but we praise God that now he has found the *"friend that sticketh closer than a brother."* To most of our servicemen, the Center is a "home-away-from-home", but to Vjellmar it was a real home, —his only home here on earth. Above all, we thank God that he made sure of an eternal home in Heaven.

"...Eye hath not seen, nor ear heard, neither have entered into the heart of man, the things which God hath prepared for them that love Him." —I Corinthians 2:9

VICTORIES

The Lord has been in our midst in wonder-working power and our hearts have burned within us as He walked with us in the way. At times we have been on the mountain-top and seen His face. Sometimes we have wanted to build three tabernacles and often we have felt as if we should take off our shoes because we were treading on holy ground. What glory to see miracles of men made new as they kneel at the feet of Jesus!

I admired Walter for his honesty as he told me that he was a Church member, but not a real Christian. He quietly listened as God spoke to his heart from His Word. There was shame and conviction written upon his countenance and he did not hesitate when I gave him an invitation to settle the question of his soul's salvation. Both prayer rooms were being used as other workers were praying with souls, so we finally found a little back room that was vacant and quiet. Tears dripped as Walter confessed his sin and opened his heart to Jesus . . . and then he poured out his heart to God for the salvation of his family and friends. Today Walter was back with a glowing face, bringing four of his buddies to us that we might tell them of Jesus and His love. Until about 11 P.M. last night, Walter was a lost, hell-bound sinner. . . . In a moment, Jesus made him a child of God and today he is a missionary! Wonderful isn't it?

One day a young man came in and as he gazed around, he said, "This is the place. I'm sure this is the place alright. I'm looking for a religious lady who won't let anybody get out without talking to them about God." We cherish these simple words as a compliment, pleasing to God, Who has called us to be His witnesses. This young man had a problem of sin in his heart and the burden had become too heavy to bear. That day he gave his heart to Christ and found that burdens are lifted at Calvary. Thank God for thirsty souls! Here is another. After pleading with many who seemingly have no concern for their own souls, but who trample the precious blood of Jesus beneath their feet, what a joy it is to meet these! Melvin was this kind and I enjoyed so much witnessing to him. Moving his chair closer, he strained to catch every word, not wanting to miss the message Jesus had for him. Several times his buddy tried vigorously to get him to leave, but Melvin completely ignored him because the story of Jesus and Heaven was sweet to his soul and there was a thirst in his heart that he knew only Jesus could quench. What a refreshing experience it was for me to kneel with this fine young man, who fell at the feet of Jesus saying, "I didn't know. I didn't know dear Jesus how to be saved until today. . . ."

Glancing at the luggage and the large familiar envelope that contained his orders, I knew the young man reading his pocket book was shipping out. Because he was very careful to keep the cover hid from my view as I spoke to him about Jesus, I knew the book must be a licentious one. How stoutly he declared that he kept the ten commandments! When I asked him about just the first one, he argued that he loved God with ALL his heart, ALL his mind and ALL his soul. I laid my Bible beside his filthy book and let God speak to his heart as I turned from verse to verse. *"Is not my Word like as a fire? saith the Lord; and like a hammer that breaketh the rock in pieces"* (Jeremiah 23:29). Suddenly this young man literally flung his book to the floor and cried out in disgust, "Oh, I hate myself. I'm full of sin and I've been so much worse since I've been in this Air Force. I hate myself!" In the prayer room, God broke those bonds of iniquity and set the captive free. God gave him a new heart, a new face, a new language and a new Book. As he left the Center his face was beaming as he joyfully tucked the Testament and the little book, "Now That I Believe" under his arm and said to us, "You pulled me out of the fires of Hell."

How can I describe Gus to you? It was years ago, but I still remember how our old model T Ford spit and sputtered and smoked when my brother tried to run it on kerosene instead of gas. Gus reminded me of that Ford. My first glimpse of him was in the prayer room, snooping around in the literature placed there for the Christian workers. He was a little quick-tempered fellow with lots of sputter and what a time I had trying to give him the gospel! As if possessed of the Devil, he spit and sputtered at me until in the flesh I wanted to flee and speak to somebody who was a little sweeter . . . , but I took his insults for about an hour because God made me conscious of the worth of his soul. We were still in the prayer room and I was almost spent when we walked out, Gus still breathing out insults. The Center was full of boys and he made quite a spectacle of himself and me too. Rev. Crockett was at the counter and after quietly observing for a time, he began to speak to Gus. Frankly, I was very glad to be relieved of him. For an hour or so they stood at the counter and talked and to my amazement, I could see that Gus was simmering down. Later on to my even greater amazement, I saw them disappear into the prayer room! When Gus came out, he was a NEW man! Immediately he rushed to me and gripped with the wonder of his conversion, he bubbled over, "I'm saved! I really am! Oh, I want you to forgive me for the way I talked to you. You were right, I was filled with the Devil but in there, YOU SHOULD HAVE HEARD ME PRAY!!! I know you can't believe it, but I'm really saved!" In a little meeting later on, one of the Christian boys gave his testimony and ended by saying, ". . . and I thank God that I have seen God's power in here today." Gus, still confounded with the wonder of his conversion, immediately burst forth with, "You're just not kidding!" and then he went on to tell how God saved him and changed his heart.

These stories thrill the heart, but we could tell you many many more stories that would break your heart. The hearts of men are growing harder and we hear the laughs, the jeers, the sneers; we listen to the scoffers who are walking in their lusts. I read of the last days in II Tim. 3:1-5 and a stillness grips my heart and sobers me. *"This know also, that in the last days perilous times shall come. For men shall be lovers of their own selves, covetous, boasters, proud, blasphemers, disobedient to parents, unthankful, unholy, without natural affection, truce-breakers, false accusers, incontinent, fierce, despisers of those that are good, traitors, heady, highminded, lovers of pleasures more than lovers of God; having a form of godliness, but denying the power thereof: from such turn away."* "Beloved, these days are upon us and I hear Jesus say, 'Take ye heed! Don't be engrossed with the cares of this life, so that day come upon you unawares.' He is near! Even at the door!" Oh, if we believe it, let us prove it by going out to rescue the perishing, pulling them out of the fires of Hell. Do we really care?

Dear old Peter wrote, *"Yea, I think it meet, as long as I am in this tabernacle, to stir you up by putting you in remembrance"* (II Pet. 1:13). How often we Christians need to be "stirred up!" On the wall in my little office is an article. I put it there because I knew it would do me good to read it often. It was sent to each of the Center workers, months ago, by the Director of our work, Rev. Crockett. This article reveals his heart. What an example he is to us who work for him . . . stirring us up and encouraging our hearts to give of our best to Jesus. Each of us thank God daily for such a leader. I am not sure, but I can imagine this article was written along the road, traveling the long miles from Center to Center . . . as God talked to his heart about the ministry entrusted to his care. At least I know God gave it to him for me. How often, as I read it, have I been challenged anew to be a better servant of the Lord Jesus. It is for this reason I share it with you . . . with a prayer that it will "stir you up" to care for the souls of men more than the cares of this life. In part it reads:

". . . In the article you write for the Good News Bulletin, please put some thought, time and prayer into it. Sweat some blood into it. Nothing comes easy that does much good. Not a newspaper article, but a fresh experience from the Lord that touched your own heart. . . . Don't dry up with others. Drive your roots deep enough to strike moisture. God's resources are inexhaustible . . . . Let us buckle up for a big year of winning souls to Jesus. Memorize some new Bible verses. Take time to pray, and drive your love roots a little deeper. The time is short. Death stares folk in the face, AND THERE ARE SO FEW WHO CARE OR KNOW HOW TO SHOW THE WAY OF SALVATION. This is our day and a challenging day it is. In the flesh I would like to quit but since I don't know how, nor do I want to fail the Lord, I am going to dig a little bit deeper and work just a little harder, die in the attempt if need be. In other words let us push together for a bigger and better work, thinking that this may be the last year."

Just In Case

"If I knew that tomorrow there would be
*   no dawn on earth for me;*
That I would go in the dark of night
*   into eternity—*
I would do so many things for those I love.
My hands should not be empty
*   As I meet my God above!*

So— Just in case I might be viewing
*   Morning in celestial skies,*
Lord, send me to those who need my love today,
*   For, otherwise,*
The night may close a door
*   On words I meant to say,*
And morning find my empty house—
*   With me away."*

41

JUANITA FINDS CHRIST PRECIOUS

". . . Her sins, which are many, are forgiven; . . ."
—Luke 7:47

As she came in the door I realized what kind of a girl she was, —the kind we are careful about having in the Center, — the kind that follow the army camps around. I greeted her and she sat down in a chair by the radio, her eyes staring into space. I studied her for awhile. She was thin and pale and sad looking, but a pretty girl, too, with beautiful blond hair. I went over and spoke to her and said, "Are you a Christian?" Rather sadly she said, "No, but I would like to be." I took my Bible and turning from Scripture to Scripture, showed her the Lord Jesus Christ, the One who loved her and wanted to save her, cleanse her, and give her a new life that would bring praise to His Name. It wasn't long before Juanita was on her knees in the prayer room, sobbing her way to Jesus. When she finished praying she continued to sob, saying, "I'm such a sinner. You don't know what kind of a girl I am." Then she told me of her life of deep sin since she was a girl of thirteen. She was only seventeen years old now. She had just gotten out of the hospital where she had lost her baby. . . . It was a sad story but we rejoiced greatly that God had forgiven and cleansed her in the precious blood of Christ. Juanita came in often in the next few days and we prayed together, read God's Word together, and talked about the goodness and mercy of God. What a change in her life, even her very countenance! She often braided her beautiful blond hair around her head, and it seemed to halo her face, which took on a heavenly glow. A Christian who met her exclaimed to me, "She almost looks like an angel!"

42

One day she came in and I was dealing with a soldier about his soul. He knew he needed Christ but was saying, "No, not today." Juanita listened and her heart was moved. As I turned to leave him, she shyly came over to his chair and sweetly told him how Jesus had saved her just a few days before and how precious it was to be ready to meet the Lord. It was a joy to my heart to hear her testify for her new-found Christ and I could see that the Holy Spirit was speaking to his heart. As a result the soldier was saved that day. As she left, she walked out the door, and then as if she had an afterthought, she opened the door again. With deep expression of sorrow she said to me, "Dorothy, I wish someone had told me about Jesus before I got so deep in sin. . . ." I looked up from my writing and smiled to her. She hesitated a moment, smiled back and walked down the street.

Several days passed and I began to wonder why she didn't come back to see me. Her home was in Texas and I knew she had sent to her parents for money and was going back as soon as she received it, but I didn't think she would leave without saying good-bye. One day her landlady called me up and said, "Do you remember Juanita?" I said, "Yes, I do and I've been wondering about her." She began to weep, saying, "They shipped her body back to Texas this morning. . . . She never got well after having the baby. . . ." This lady was not a Christian, but she added, "I'm so glad you helped her get back to God. The day she was saved there, she came home and got down on her knees before me and said, 'Mrs. Beck, please try and forgive me. All I have been telling you about myself are lies but I was saved today and I'm going to live for Jesus now.' " The landlady continued, "Since then she was the sweetest girl. . . . I loved her as my own daughter . . . ."

As I heard the news of Juanita's death, tears rolled down my cheeks and my heart was so heavy because in that short time I had learned to love her, my sister in Christ. Yet in my sorrow there was rejoicing and grateful thanks to God. I

43

knew Juanita was with her Saviour, in that wonderful home He had prepared for her. —And not only that, but she did not meet her Saviour empty-handed! She had a precious soul to present to Him.

Dear Christian friend, has the Lord spoken to your heart? Today, if God should suddenly call YOU home, would you have to meet Him empty-handed or would you hear His, "Well done. . . ." ?

> *"Must I go, and empty-handed,*
> *Thus my dear Redeemer meet?*
> *Not one day of service give Him,*
> *Lay no trophy at His feet?*
> *Must I go, and empty-handed?*
> *Must I meet my Saviour so?*
> *Not one soul with which to greet Him:*
> *Must I empty-handed go?*

FULLNESS OF JOY

"They that sow in tears shall reap in joy."   *—Psalm 126:5*

This was a message from God to my heart today and I want to tell you about it. I was making pies this morning . . . (sixteen of them) for "our boys." We love to do these little special things to remind them that we love them and that this is "home." Yet we must be very careful that we do not get so busy doing "things" that we cannot speak to these precious souls about their need of the Lord Jesus. How often God has heard our prayer to speed our hands that we might do the work quickly and thus, have time to witness! As I rolled out the dough, I could see the Center begin to fill with boys, and there was a sob in my heart. I wanted to be out there telling them about Jesus! I prayed as I hurried and finished at just the right time! The Lord was bringing five precious boys my way and as they enjoyed the coffee and cookies, they asked how we provided all this free for the men. It is always thrilling for me to tell how God provides our every need in answer to prayer . . . how God touches the hearts of His children to give because they love the Lord Jesus and these boys in service. This seemed to touch their hearts and I continued to speak about the goodness of God and how He willingly gave His Son that we might be saved. As I poured out my heart, longing for them to listen and accept Christ, one by one they walked away until there was only one remaining to hear the words of Jesus. My heart was strangely moved in compassion for them and their awful condition. Raising my voice a bit so they could all hear I asked, "Fellows, why did you walk away when I began to talk to you about your need of the Lord Jesus? I could talk to you about other things and you would all stand here and listen. I was telling you about the One who loved you so much that he came all the way from Heaven's glory and gave His life that you might have everlasting life.... You left me talking to the air, except for this one young man. Fellows, if you don't learn to love him and talk about Him now, how would you feel in Heaven in His very presence...?" As I continued to speak from my heart, the Lord was doing a wonderful thing. One by one he was bringing them back! It really was wonderful... and they listened to the voice of God, some with bowed heads of shame, sniffing back the tears. As Jesus knocked at their hearts, I invited them to go to the prayer room with me and ask the Lord Jesus to save them and take His rightful place on the throne in their hearts. This time, instead of being ashamed of them and their actions, I had great respect for their manliness. Showing no embarrassment or concern as to what the others might do, each one immediately looked at me and expressed a desire to accept the Lord Jesus as his Saviour. It was so blessed to kneel with those five sin-burdened boys and hear them call upon the Lord Jesus. Tears of joy and sorrow mingled and dripped to the floor. Five hearts were washed white as snow in the blood of Jesus. Afterward as we rejoiced and fellowshipped in the things of the Lord, they kept thanking me for caring enough for their souls to rebuke and then plead with them. What a wonderful change when Jesus comes into our hearts! As I write this, my heart is flooded with joy. *"In Thy presence is fulness of joy"*... and I have just been in His presence where He has performed five miracles of redeeming grace. Praise His worthy Name!

One afternoon I happened to notice a young negro airman standing in the prayer room just looking around. After a while I looked in and said, "This is the place where sinners meet Jesus, —the place where we pray with boys who want Jesus to come into their hearts. How about you? Do you want Jesus to come into your heart and save you?" I was astonished a bit when he replied, "Yes mam, I sure would like it. I feel Jesus all around me in here but I can't say He is in my heart. My mother sent me a Bible and I have been reading it. . . ." Sensing that his heart was prepared, I suggested, "Let's just kneel down here in the Lord's presence and look at a few Scripture verses." He immediately knelt with me and soon this precious lad was mopping his brow and rubbing his sweating hands together as God brought conviction to his heart. Very simply he confessed his sin and invited the Lord Jesus in to save him. Afterward he was so happy and grateful, saying, "This is what I have wanted to do for a long time but I didn't know how to go about it.

——Another weekend is almost over. A goodly number have come to Jesus, but many have gone out rejecting Christ. At almost midnight, weary in body after hours and hours of witnessing, we turn out some of the lights and over a sandwich, speak with heavy hearts of those who defied God and went out to continue in sin. As if to ease and lift our burden a bit, God drew our attention to a heavenly strain. Our precious Christian boys, in the semi-darkness, were still gathered around the piano singing:

"Oh how I love Him, Saviour and Friend,
How shall my praises ever find end—
Through endless ages, on Heaven's shore
My tongue shall praise Him, forevermore!
Blessed Redeemer! Precious Redeemer!
Seems now I see Him on Calvary's tree—
Wounded and bleeding, for sinners pleading
Blind and unheeding, Dying for me. . . ."

Moved with the wonder of God's love that had so changed these boys, so they now sang with such devotion to the Saviour, Brother Crockett said, "Listen— Did you ever hear anything sweeter than that?" As I listened, I was near moved to tears and I could only say, "No. Never!"

With lifted spirits, we closed the Center, breathing the prayer, "Thank you, Lord for the privilege of serving You here."

AN INDIAN CHIEF

"Another called, another brought
Dear Master, to Thy feet!
Oh, where are words to tell the joy,
So wonderful and sweet!
Oh, where are words to give Thee thanks,
To praise with angel throng!
Who even now are pouring forth,
A new and joyful song."

How we praise the Lord! Another soul won't have to go to Hell! God has spoken to an Indian Chief and said, *"I have... called thee from the chief men ... and said unto thee, Thou art my servant; I have chosen thee, ..."* (Isa. 41:9).

For three days straight, at about 4 P.M. an Air Force man came into the Center and seemed to enjoy the quiet Christian atmosphere. This man was a real American, —A full-blooded American Indian, and a M/Sgt. in the service of his country. The first time I spoke to him about his soul, he was gracious to listen, but made no response. Yesterday he came again, and the Holy Spirit in my heart was telling me that I "must needs" speak to him again about his soul. This would be our last opportunity. Tomorrow he was getting his discharge, leaving this base and going back to the Indian Reservation in Oregon ... having been chosen to be the Chief of his tribe. I realized what a trophy he would be for Jesus, reaching his own tribe with the gospel.

The Lord wonderfully opened the way, and again, I found myself very freely telling the story of God's redeeming grace, to this dear man. I sensed in the way he listened so intently, that this time his ears were hearing the voice of Jesus. He listened long and patiently as I gave forth the message that I well knew God was bringing so wonderfully to my lips to deliver.

Two hours must have ticked away, unnoticed by either of us. "Sergeant, you must not put it off any longer," I urged. "Wouldn't you like to go into the prayer room and kneel down before the Lord Jesus and receive Him as your Lord and Saviour? He wants to wash away your sins in His precious blood and make you His own son. Will you do it today, if I help you?" I knew he was going to speak, and after a few moments of silence, in his quiet impressive way, he said, "I was wanting to ask you to pray with me. I am like you were twenty-one years ago, lost from Jesus Christ. . . . Today I believe He has called me to His heart." I knew this was a statement of honest and deep conviction.

The Lord seemed to overshadow the little prayer room and fill it with His holy Presence as this big Indian Chief knelt down, humbling himself under the mighty hand of God. When I asked him to call upon the Lord, I realized there was a struggle going on in his heart, and his whole body was trembling. Suddenly, he lifted his head high, and with his hands reaching up toward Heaven, he began to pray in a broken voice, and his very soul seemed to cry out to the great God of Heaven, for mercy and pardon. We were on holy ground, and it was good to be there.

The Chief's face, which had been almost expressionless before we knelt, broke into a sweet smile from time to time, as we looked into the Word, and God opened his eyes to see and believe the precious promises. As we enjoyed the Lord and feasted on His Word, we were not conscious of time, but when we arose from our knees and came out of the prayer room, we were startled to find it dark! Over four hours had passed since we began to talk about Jesus! . . .But they were not wasted. . . . These were hours that will forever be recorded in eternity.

"Another voice to 'tell it out',
What great things Thou hast done,
Another life to live for Thee,
Another witness won."

FISHING FOR MEN

Today has been a difficult one for me and it has been a fight to stand against the wiles of Satan. I am praising the Lord tonight that we who love Jesus are not ignorant of Satan's devices.... How we need to resist him and put on the whole armour of God to *"stand"* and *"withstand,"* in the evil day. *"Thanks be to God, which giveth us the victory through our Lord Jesus Christ"* (I Cor. 15:57).

Tonight I had a longing in my heart to share Jesus with several airmen who stood at the counter drinking coffee and munching "prayer cookies." (Prayer cookies are the ones a Christian mother makes. As she bakes them, she prays that as the boys eat them, they will hear the gospel and receive Christ as Saviour.) Five boys, two of whom had been drinking, gathered around to listen. I witnessed to them about their need of Christ to save and change their lives. They listened attentively, yet, one by one they left without Jesus. My heart was a little heavy . . . but I had noticed a Sergeant come in while we were talking. Even though he sat at a distant table, I knew he was listening and under deep conviction. I walked over and presented him with a gospel tract, "The Life That Satisfies," and asked him if he were a real Christian, saved and sure of Heaven. He said, "No, but this is why I came in tonight. I came in for you to help me." It was a real privilege to take the Word of God and explain to this seeking soul the way to Heaven. Even here Satan fought for his soul, but after struggling for two hours the Lord won the victory and sweet peace flooded his soul.

Then the Lord added another blessing. An airman was

standing at the counter and I recognized a familiar face . . .
one of the five boys I had spoken to earlier, the fellow who
had said he was a Christian Scientist. Gary was under
conviction and the Holy Spirit of God brought him back. We
knelt in the little prayer room and Gary was washed in the
blood of Christ. He just walked into the office while I was
typing this and said, "I would like to say one thing and that
is that this place is sure doing what it is supposed to do. I'm
really glad I walked in here and was saved tonight." Here is
a word of testimony from Gary himself, just a babe in Christ,
saved thirty minutes ago:

"Today I walked into the Service Center a sinner, but
unknowingly. What brought me here I cannot
explain. I talked with some airmen about religion
and Dorothy Myers was telling us that Christ is the
only way to live a full unsinful life. She said that if I
did not take Him into my heart, a sinful life would be
my reward. This happened in the early evening.
When I walked out to mail some letters, all I had on
my mind was Christ. I was alone and in a daze. God
knew I was a seeking sinner. The Holy Spirit came to
me to help me see the light. God was talking to me by
bringing back memories of my college days and
Christian friends who spoke to me there. I had to be
reborn and receive Christ as my Saviour. I came back
to the Center and began talking to another sinner.
After he left, Miss Myers asked me to let Christ do my
saving. I went into the prayer room with her and
prayed and let the Lord Jesus save me on this 21st
day of July. May I thank the everlasting hand of God
for bringing me back in the second time. To me this
was the most unexplainable thing that has ever
happened. Even my work in life is answered. After
the U.S. Air Force I am going into mission work
because I feel God wants me to serve Him. Oh! what a
miracle happened to me tonight! I never thought
such a wonderful thing could happen. I pray tonight

for all those who are still sinners and hope God's love will help more people to see the light. Amen." —Gary

"O sing unto the Lord a new song; for He hath done marvelous things: His right hand, and His holy arm, hath gotten Him the VICTORY" (Ps. 98:1).

Many of the stories in this book were written up as they happened, and as you can imagine, many of them have wonderful sequels I would like to add, —But time or space do not permit me to do so; however, I felt I just had to share a little more about Gary as He grew to love Jesus and the souls of men more and more.

The next Saturday after he was saved, Gary came in. The Christian young people were enjoying the Center, helping me witness and care for the others. In the course of the day I found myself witnessing to three men, one a Jew, one a Catholic, and the other an unsaved Church member. The three together were a little too much to handle as they began to get loud and a bit out of hand. All the Christian young people, including Gary, drew close to listen. God is never glorified in an argument of this kind and I felt each of the boys should be witnessed to separately. After awhile I turned my attention to just one of the men. As I witnessed, I noticed Gary had sort of "cornered" the loudest of the three men, and in a stammering, but intense way, was urging him to turn from sin to Jesus. Late that night, after the day was all over and the Christians were getting ready to go back to the base, Gary came to say good-bye to me. To encourage him, I said, "Gary, it was good to see you witness to that fellow tonight." In his slow, thoughtful way, he replied, "Well, I felt I should say something . . . I don't know much but I know more than he does. . . . He is so lost. Then I felt something stirring around and around inside me, —that's the Holy Spirit, isn't it?, —and I thought, I just have to tell this man something, so I said a few words about Christ. . . ."

The next Saturday Gary was in and it was one of those wonderful days when Heaven came down. The blessed Holy

Spirit of God was working and about fifteen of our young Christians, and I, were witnessing. (That day twenty-six precious souls bowed the knee and heart to Jesus.) One young unsaved airman sat at a chair and got desperately under conviction, just hearing the witnessing and rejoicing. Finally he rushed up to Gary and cried out, "Oh, I want to be saved! Please help me!" Gary later told me about it. He said, "I was just saved myself and didn't have any idea how I could help him, so I looked around for someone who could. Everybody else was busy witnessing. I was scared to death he wouldn't be saved so I thought I would take him into the prayer room like you did me. We knelt down and he was just crying. I didn't know what to do. Then I saw this little book on the prayer bench and it was opened to the flames of Hell fire. I pointed to the flames and said, 'You don't want to go there, do you?' He said, 'No, I don't want to go there.' So I read to him the Scriptures under the flames and it was real good, so I just read the whole book to him and then he kept crying and prayed until the Lord saved him. I also prayed a little prayer to Jesus Christ for him, like you did for me. . . ." Gary introduced me to the boy and he was rejoicing in the Saviour.

Gary was utterly amazed that God would use an insignificant fellow, like him, to lead a soul to Christ!!! It was very late and all the other Christians said good-bye and left but Gary seemed not to notice. He was on "cloud nine"! He just stood at the counter as if in a daze, contemplating on this wonderful thing that God had done. Finally he turned to me and with deep emotion, said, "If God is going to do that for me, maybe I should get some Scripture verses that I can use. . . ." I said, "Gary, I think that would be a good thing to do." Finally he left, saying, "I've got a lot of praying to do."

The next Saturday Gary came in and as we talked, he noticed a young man reading a magazine, and he asked me, "Has anyone talked to him yet?" I answered, "No, I don't think so." He said, "I will." I watched. Approaching the boy, Gary said, "Hello. Do you know much about being saved?"

The boy looked up from his reading, and acted as if he didn't really understand what Gary had said. Gary hesitated and then, haltingly, tried again. "Well, if you were to die today, do you know where you would go?" The boy shook his head "No," so Gary continued, "The Bible says, *'the wages of sin is death,'* and that means. . . ." He didn't finish because I don't think he knew how to explain it. He thought a moment and said, "Wait a minute." The boy seemed very interested and patiently waited. Gary walked across the room, got his Bible and took out two sheets of fine-lined notebook paper. Kneeling beside the boy, he spread the papers on the floor. I moved closer to see what was written on it. It was filled with references from the Bible. One group of verses was on sin and it's consequences, another group of verses on how Jesus shed His blood to cleanse the sinner, and another group of Scripture references on how to believe and receive Jesus as Saviour. Not being familiar with the Bible, after each verse he had the page number, such as: Romans 10:13, page 309, etc. Gary began at the top of the paper, found the page, then the verse, pointed it out to his listener, and said, "Read that." The boy read it aloud. Then Gary would do the same with the next Scripture, and the next, until he had gone through both pages of approximately fifty or sixty verses. It took a very long time but both boys were patient and extremely engrossed in the Word of God. I had been called away with other duties, but my heart was thrilled to see Gary leading this young man to the prayer room. Well, in the few months Gary was stationed here, God used him and those Scriptures to lead many many more precious souls to the Saviour.

Gary was interested in Jesus and the souls of man. Little else mattered. One day he came in and walked around, looking at everyone who was in the Center. In a disappointed voice he lamented, "It's no good at all in here today. Everybody's saved."

Someone has said that while older Christians hold back from witnessing, to make sure they have just the right approach, the right words, the right time, etc., the new Christian, filled with the love of Jesus, just plunges into witnessing, breaking all these rules, but they are having the souls. From my observation, I believe this is a fairly accurate statement.

It never ceases to amaze me how wonderfully God will use any of His children, even a new-born babe, if only that child surrenders completely to the will of his loving Heavenly Father. *"And He said to them all, If any man will come after Me, let him deny himself, and take up his cross daily, and follow Me"* (Luke 9:23). Dear reader, if you are a redeemed child of God, surrender all to Jesus, —take up your cross and follow Him. Only then will the Blessed Holy Spirit begin His work through you. He gives the vision, the burning love, the wisdom, the compassion, the unction, the boldness, the message, ——ALL we need to reach the lost for Christ.

Some years ago I was attending our annual Missionary Conference at our San Antonio, Texas Center. Very late one night, after the Center was closed, Brother Crockett took a group of us in his car for a tour around the city. He drove and drove, pointing out places of interest, until he finally stopped the car on a high hill, overlooking that vast city, and said to us, "Now, that is San Antonio." What we saw was beautiful and breath-taking. As I looked at that great, beautiful array of lights, God began to talk to my heart. The vast majority of those people, people for whom Jesus died, were lost and still on their way to Hell. . . . Then God seemed to point out something else to me, —here and there the lights were going out. One here, —one there, —one up there, —one back here. Could it be that this is what God sees in our lives as He looks down from Heaven? —Are our lights for Jesus going out. . . ? Oh may God move upon our hearts with such compassion for the lost that we will kneel at His blessed feet, confessing our sin, yielding our lives, our lips, our all to Him. Can we make this this wonderful old hymn our prayer today?

"Take my life, and let it be   Consecrated, Lord, to Thee;
Take my hands, and let them move   At the impulse of Thy love,

At the impulse of Thy love.

Take my feet, and let them be   Swift and beautiful for Thee;
Take my voice, and let me sing,   Always, only, for my King,
Always, only, for my King.

Take my silver and my gold,   Not a mite would I with-hold;
Take my moments and my days,   Let them flow in ceaseless praise,
Let them flow in ceaseless praise.

Take my will, and make it Thine,   It shall be no longer mine;
Take my heart, it is Thine own;   It shall be Thy royal throne,
It shall be Thy royal throne."

BILL AND RUSS

"He that abideth in Me, and I in him, the same bringeth forth <u>*much fruit*</u>*: .... Herein is my Father glorified, that ye bear* <u>*much fruit*</u>*; .... and that your joy might be full. ...."*

Turn in your Bible, read all of John 15 and let Jesus' words find a lodging place in your heart.

As I bubbled over with joy, telling thrilling stories of souls finding Christ, a visiting lady said to me, "I'm ashamed to tell you, but it has been so long since a soul walked the isle in our Church to be saved, that I can't remember when. . . ." How tragic and sad, —because God is not glorified when souls are not saved, —and our joy is not full unless we are winning the lost to Jesus. A healthy apple tree bears apples and a healthy Christian produces other Christians.

We have found the promises in John 15 to be a living verity. This has been a fruitful and joyful month. We have sensed greatly the prayers of God's people and felt the eyes and heart of God upon us, and this place, as we have reaped a harvest of precious souls for Jesus. Our joy has been full, strengthening and encouraging us to abide in Christ and to continue in bearing witness of His saving grace.

Space is so limited here. Only in eternity, when time shall be no more, can we share fully all these joys with you who give and pray. How I look forward to that great day! Today I have asked God to help me tell some of these experiences to make them "live" for you, bringing joy to your heart and glorifying Him.

Just thinking about our "new" Bill brings great joy to my heart. He is filled and overflowing with the wonderful new life he has found in Christ. As we witness for Jesus, Bill prays and anxiously awaits their decision. If it is to the prayer room, he has a quick, fervent response, such as, "Beautiful! Great! Best thing he ever did!" If a man rejects Christ, his response is the direct opposite and comes from a sorrowful heart, "Blind! Throwing his life away, just throwing his life away! If only he knew. . . ."

Being around Bill, even we older Christians experience a little revival in our own souls! His last words as he left late last night were, "Boy I'll never forget to say a prayer for every one of the boys who go out those doors without Jesus! That's for sure!"

Two weeks ago, Bill could have cared less! He came in, a rough and tumble, arrogant and boastful sinner from Boston. His home was broken up when he was a child and he was left to romp the streets. He learned to steal for a living and ate out of garbage cans, —dodging the police and sleeping where they could not find him. At the age of seventeen, he enlisted in the Air Force. He lied, telling the recruiter he was eighteen years old so he would be accepted. As we witnessed to him the first time, he quickly left, thinking to himself, "I've SURE got the wrong place!" —But the Lord brought him back and he kicked against the pricks of God's Word, making quite a scene in the Center and pouring out remarks such as, "Just give me a bottle and I'm happy . . . etc." Remembering that he had been kicked around all his life, an outcast from his home and having to make his own way from an early age, I felt an urge to present the great love and compassion of God to Bill. *"If father and mother forsake thee, then the Lord will take thee up."* By his silence it was very evident that love was winning, so finally I gave Bill the tract, "God's Simple Plan of Salvation," urged him to read it and then come back and talk to me. Miserable with conviction of sin, he would read awhile, then stare into space. Finally he came back and with only a few more words,

Bill yielded his whole heart and life to Jesus. As God promised, his whole life changed, even his countenance. For the first time in his life he is attending a Bible-believing Church and loves it. His new little Testament is cherished. It's Words are sweeter than honey to his soul. Pray for Bill, especially as he leaves soon, but with a desire to reach his family for Jesus.

A nice looking, gentle-mannered young lad was reading a booklet, "What It Means to Be Saved," and was looking up the references in my Bible. As I introduced myself and asked about his soul's salvation, he revealed that he was not saved but was seeking to know Christ. "Do you know the Roman Rogue to salvation?" he asked. For some time I was puzzled as to what he meant but after several questions I found he meant, Roman Road to salvation. (I had heard of this before. It's when a person uses verses in Romans to point a person to Christ.) Russ had heard of this in a Bible Camp.

We opened God's Word and began to point out Scriptures to show Russ his lost condition and how Jesus wanted to save him. Earnestly he listened and the Lord spoke to his heart. As I was extending Jesus' gracious invitation and inviting him to the prayer room, suddenly Russ fainted and fell straight backwards to the floor with a loud thud. Seeing him lying there, pale and unconscious, we were shocked to action and administered first-aid. After an anxious time, he began to revive and we were able to get him to a couch to lie down. While still shaken from this experience, God spoke to my heart that this fainting spell was a trick of Satan to keep this precious boy from Jesus. Wanting the Lord to have the victory, I knelt by Russ' side and prayed. Then I spoke to him and he, too, recognized that Satan was fighting desperately for his soul, saying that there seemed to be a wall that separated him from coming to Christ. Urging him to call upon the Lord and get it settled, Russ said, "I want to— Now." Immediately he folded his hands in prayer, closed his eyes and began to pray, confessing his sin and inviting Christ into his heart. When he finished a sweet smile broke out upon his face and in an awed whisper said, "It was so easy! That's all there is to it. I'm saved. Thank you God, I am saved!" After a prayer of thanksgiving and sharing a few Scripture promises with him, I left saying I would help him more in the Bible later on. I felt he should rest awhile.

Several hours later I looked in on Russ and he was sitting on the side of the couch. When he saw me, he said, "Things were so vague to me when I prayed before. In case I wasn't sincere enough, I want to ask Jesus to save me again and make real sure." Once again we prayed and the joy of the Lord brought God's peace to his heart.

Sunday Russ was back, beaming for the Lord. After Bible Study Sunday afternoon in the Center, he went to Church with the other Christian boys. As they stopped in here for a snack before going back to the base, I admonished them to live for Christ this week and to do and say what they could for Him, even if only a little, that others could be saved. Monday Russ came in and said, "You know I was thinking about what you said and I wanted God to use me. This morning in the barracks, I had a desire to pray, —to really get alone with God and pray, —but all the boys were around, so I went over by the window and knelt down and prayed to God. It was so wonderful. God was so near and I didn't even hear the boys and all the noise in the barracks." When Russell got up from his knees, a boy was standing by him and he said, "You were praying, weren't you? I want to have a long talk with you sometime. I am far away from God but I want to be a Christian."

Russ is continuing to grow in grace and reads everything about Jesus he can get his hands on, desiring to be used of God to reach his buddies for Christ.

In closing, I want to share this with you. One night a young man came in who had tried twice to commit suicide, was on drugs, etc. When I saw his misery, I said, "These should be the happiest years of your life. . . ." He responded with, "I have a lot of friends, but I don't believe any of them

61

are really happy, —but WHO CARES?" How good it was to tell him that there are those who care. JESUS cares for his poor lost soul and gave His life to deliver him from Satan's clutches. WE care and spend long hours pleading with sinners. YOU dear ones care and pray so faithfully and give sacrificially that they may be saved and have the joy of the Lord. God help us to pray and care, even more, for those yet outside the fold of Christ.

> *"My soul was groping in the night*
> *Of darkness drear, by sin ensnared*
> *But light broke forth and hope returned*
> *My doubts are gone because you cared."*

THE DEAF HEAR HIS VOICE

"My soul thirsteth for God, for the LIVING God: . . ."
                                                    —Ps. 42:2

As I unlocked the office door this morning, I turned and opened the door to the prayer room also. I love our little prayer room and I am always filled with a little reverence and awe when I look upon this place where our Lord has heard and answered the heart-cries of so many who have come to Him in their need. My heart was moved as I stood there this morning . . . "O God," I prayed, "Use this little prayer room a lot today. . . ."

A short time later God began to answer that prayer by leading two servicemen into the Center. As I spoke to them I found that neither was a real Christian, and one professed to be a Buddhist. How wonderful to tell them of a living Christ! They listened for over an hour as I presented to them the precious truths from God's Holy Word. The Lord had so broken them to see their sin and need of Him, that when I asked if they had room in their hearts for the Lord Jesus Christ, one swallowed as he fought to keep the tears back and nodded his head. —The other opened his mouth but no words came so he looked to me with a pleading expression on his face which told me he wanted Jesus, too. As they knelt with me in the prayer room, once again the Lord met us and made His abode in the hearts of these two young airmen as they called unto Him to save them from their sins.

About an hour later I rejoiced to see Stella, our Christian WAF, leading two boys to that little prayer room. —We sense the Lord's presence and blessing in a wonderful way today.

Soon we are leading another seeking sinner to the prayer room . . . then another, and another and another . . . until we count ten precious souls who have knelt before the Lord Jesus Christ, realizing they were lost, hell-bound sinners, and who called upon the name of the Lord for salvation. We only wish you who pray and share the burdens could have been here with us today to bask in these heavenly blessings as God drew so very near.

Picking up a pencil and piece of paper I wrote, "I am a Christian and I like to help people. Are you a Christian? Have you let Jesus come into your heart to wash your sins away?" I passed this to the young man who stood silent before me. He read it and took out a pencil and wrote, "I am stone deaf since my birth. I wish I know how. Never go to church. No use for me to go because they talk too fast for deaf to understand." Back and forth we wrote until the top of the counter was covered with sheets of paper. He read many Bible verses I pointed out to him.

". . . Even the deaf can hear the voice of Jesus. Don't you hear the voice of Jesus speaking to your heart? Won't you listen to Jesus and ask Him into your heart to wash away your sins. . . ?" I quickly scribbled. A real struggle was going on in his heart and many many times he refused Jesus but finally as he wiped sweat from his brow, he wrote, "Look like I give up. You win. Why you care for me?" After more conversation by notes, we prayed. Then one look into his beaming face told me the struggle was over and he had really given his heart to Christ. Quickly he reached for a paper and wrote, "I thank you what you did to soften the hard heart of mine. Look like my heart been beating too fast. I prayed and opened my heart to Jesus. He knock. I'm glad I did. You are right. No one ever care to explain to me before. Why you care, may I ask?"

This was a very precious but new experience for me . . . the first soul I have ever led to the Lord Jesus without uttering a word! How nearly I missed this blessing from Heaven by just giving him a gospel tract and letting him go on his way! It took four hours and ninety-two written pages, but I am so thankful to God for saving this soul. *". . . He hath done all things well: He maketh both the deaf to hear, and the dumb to speak."* Mark 7:37 —Selah!

LIVING WATER

"Whosoever drinketh of this water shall thirst again."
—John 4:13

How true these words of Jesus. A little figuring told us that we served over 800 cups of orange juice to the boys on Saturday. But how well we knew they would be back, — thirsty again!

"But whosoever drinketh of the water that I shall give him shall never thirst" (John 4:14). As we worked and witnessed, we longed to find thirsty souls, and that day we prayed with ten young men who drank of this "Living Water."

At times the Center was full of hungry, thirsty boys and it was impossible to speak to each one about Jesus, but we tried to give them a gospel tract and say a few words for the Lord. Don received his tract and heard the few words I spoke as he stood at the counter with a large group of other men. As I gave out tracts to the others in the Center I looked up to find my path blocked. This young man had stationed himself in front of me with a pitiful and pleading expression that immediately seemed to say, "Please tell me more about Jesus." I read his heart right because that was exactly what he yearned for! How eagerly he listened and then knelt in the presence of Jesus and prayed this simple prayer from his heart and soul. "Jesus, you know how I walked out of the barracks today searching for something—I didn't know what. I walked all over town, but I didn't find it there. I went in all the stores and to the U.S.O. but I didn't find it there. I didn't know what I was even searching for but it seemed like

I had to keep on searching. Then I came in this place. It seemed different and I thought, 'Maybe I will find what I am searching for in here.' Then this lady gave me this little book and talked to me about you. Then I knew this was what I was searching for. I was searching for YOU." .... Then he went on to sweetly and simply confess his sin and receive the Lord Jesus as his Saviour. The thirsty soul was quenched and the next day Don, shining and smiling for joy said to me, "Oh, I just wish I could give everyone what I have!"

Gus, himself a babe in Christ, brought in Ray, his roommate, that he might be saved. Ray was a Catholic and at first rebelled. Then admitting that he wasn't satisfied, he promised me that if God spoke to his heart, he would do what God wanted him to. Before long I realized that here was another soul, thirsting greatly, *"as the hart panteth after the waterbrooks"* (Ps. 42:1). We turned from Scripture to Scripture and Ray could hardly believe what God was opening up to him. Then I read, *"Whosoever drinketh of the water that I shall give him shall never thirst"* (John 4:14). "Ray, do you have a thirsty soul?" I asked. Great sobs shook his whole body and he cried out, "Oh, yes!" Embarrassed with his tears and trying to control them he said, "Please excuse me. I guess you don't see anything like this often." I smiled and assured him that it happened almost every day in the Center. It was such a joy to kneel beside Ray as his soul, thirsting after the living Christ, was satisfied.

I was talking to five boys about their need of the Lord Jesus, and one by one they walked away until only two remained to listen. Three more young men moved closer to listen but when they heard me quoting Scripture they began to smirk and snicker among themselves. So often we encounter this. (Ungrateful, wicked men can eat God's good food, breathe His good air . . . but he sneers in his Creator's face when He tries to bring the message of His love and redeeming grace to their hearts and minds. Only Satan could make them make such fools of themselves!) Trying to ignore them, I continued to witness to the two boys listening.

Lloyd had been saved years ago, even called to **preach**, but sin had entered his life and he was far from God. David was drinking in the words of eternal life for the first time. As we knelt in prayer, Lloyd was restored to fellowship with His Lord. The old cigarettes were tossed into the waste basket, along with the tear-stained kleenex tissues. Trembling, David sobbed his way to Jesus. We who knelt with him knew that Jesus had transformed another life. As he tried to tell us how wonderful it was, there was a great sob and tears between each word. Only another winner of souls can know the joy that welled up in my heart as I listened and looked into that tear-stained and puffed face, glowing with a glow that only comes from the touch of the Saviour's hand. Beyond all doubt, the happiest moments we spend on this old earth are those on our knees, leading souls to Jesus. Thank God for the honor and privilege!

Last night the Christian young people and I were all so weary from witnessing. It was the end of a long hard weekend. Things had quieted down in the Center and we were thinking of getting a bit of food for the body when one by one a few more boys began to straggle in. All of us felt as if we were just too tired to even try to bring another to the feet of Jesus. . . . But we know He has promised strength for our labors, and we asked Him for this, and that He would give the listeners tender receptive hearts. Oh, the greatness of God's love, not only for sinners, but for His servants! In less than an hour four new names had been recorded eternally in Heaven! So late, so weary . . . BUT GOD! We know the joy of reality when we take hold of His promises, knowing there is strength from above available to us.

In closing, let us ask God to search our hearts. How much do we really value a soul? Do we talk about the pricelessness of a human soul and then live and give as if it isn't worth very much? Honest now, how long has it been since you gave Jesus a *sacrificial* love gift? I stand ashamed. How about you? There may be only a few more days left to serve Jesus. Why not give him the treasures we have foolishly heaped together for the last days! Soon we shall hear His "come up hither" . . . These "tents" will be folded forever and we will trade them for mansions of gold. Oh, that you and I might have a few more crowns to lay at Jesus' feet!

"For ye know the grace of our Lord Jesus Christ, that, though He was rich, yet for your sakes He became poor, that ye through His poverty might be rich." II Cor. 8:9

> *"Out of this life I shall never take,*
> *Things of silver and gold I make.*
> *All that I cherish and hoard away——*
> *After I leave, on this earth must stay,*
>
> *All that I gather, and all that I keep,*
> *I must leave behind, when I fall asleep.*
> *And I often wonder, 'what shall I own*
> *In that other life when I pass alone?'*
>
> *What shall they find, and what shall they see*
> *In the soul that answers the call for me?*
> *Shall the great Judge learn when my task is through*
> *That my spirit has gathered some riches too?*
>
> *Or shall at last, it be mine to find*
> *That all I have worked for I have left behind?"*

SATAN'S FLIES

". . . for Thy Name's sake lead me, and guide me." —Ps. 31:3

Are you often bored with your life? Then perhaps you need to let the Holy Spirit upset the monotonous program that YOU set-up for yourself day after day. This morning He really upset my program! He made me late for work . . . and I am rejoicing in it! I want to share this with you.

As I hurried to get to the Center on time, the Holy Spirit prompted me to pause and *"shew forth His lovingkindness in the morning"* to Judy—a very dear serviceman's wife. The recognition of her sin and lost condition made the tears come, until they streamed down her face. As she sobbed, she listened and heard of the Saviour's love and the power in His blood to cleanse and renew. When I knew the Holy Spirit had made the way clear to Judy, I paused, waiting for her to answer. Very simply and clearly she said, "I want Jesus to come into my heart and save me now." Immediately we both went to our knees and that little humble spot became an altar, as tears dripped upon it. Judy offered herself to Jesus, bidding Him to enter her heart. This is why I was late for work . . . and rejoicing in it.

Judy and I would ask your prayers for Johnnie, her husband and a very fine, open-hearted young man with high ideals. He was very silent as he learned of Judy's salvation, and then in an awed sweetness, said, "Did you have a REVIVAL?" For a long time we three talked about Jesus. Johnnie is still outside the fold of Christ, but his heart is tender. Sensing keenly the emptiness and artificial lives of many, Johnnie is looking for something real and genuine.

He later confided in his wife, "Dorothy really does have something. Nobody would work like she does and put in the hours she does if they didn't have something." I was reminded anew of the importance of having our lives correspond with the message we bear.

The Holy Spirit upset my plans again. As I shut off the lights the old body told me that it was alright to close; the flesh was weary and so ready to quit for the day. The clock told us that it was alright to close the Center; it was the proper time—BUT . . . the Holy Spirit moved right in upon those plans and drew my attention to a young man. Why was he tarrying? Why did he suddenly pick up a Bible and begin to read in the semi-darkness? The Holy Spirit made it clear to my heart. He led me to sit down beside Jim and tell him about Jesus. Jim was seeking the Lord but groping in the dark and his attempts to live a clean life failed again and again. Once more God was showing His faithfulness in revealing Himself to those who really seek Him. The Holy Spirit was making the message clear, taking the Word and showing Jim that he could only live a life pleasing to God when Jesus was abiding in his heart.

Jim seemed overwhelmed that God would allow him to hear this wonderful news and I have never seen one strain so to hear . . . but he was being terribly distracted! It amazes me to see the things Satan uses to hinder God's message from shining into hearts! This time it was three flies . . . and at this season when they should all be gone! Again and again they would swoop down and buzz so viciously into Jim's face as he was trying so hard to catch every word I spoke. Repeatedly he brushed them away, only to have them come back more determined than ever! Finally Jim looked at me puzzled for a moment. Then in a very positive but astonished tone he exclaimed, "I believe those flies are filled with the Devil! They're trying to distract me so I can't hear what you are saying. They don't want me to hear how to be saved!" Such perception from an unsaved person is so rare, but how true his statement! The amazing thing was that after he said

71

this, the flies left immediately. It made me think! Satan only wins through deceit. He knew he could never be the victor in the battle for this soul, because his subtle attempts were known. . . Just *"as the hart panteth after the water brooks,"* so Jim's soul panted to know God, and this was the way his prayer went up to the throne. I was privileged to enjoy a little taste of Heaven . . . I was in the presence of God as he performed a miracle in Jim's heart. Jim was overwhelmed as the glorious light of the gospel flooded his heart. He was "seeing" for the first time. . . God's Word began to live for him. While he was still kneeling in the place where Jesus had saved him, I turned to John 5:24 and read the verse: *"Verily, verily, I say unto you, He that heareth My word, and believeth on Him that sent Me, hath everlasting life, and shall not come into condemnation; but is passed from death unto life."* It seemed as if Jim could not take his eyes away and he stared at these words a long time in silence. Then slowly, reverently, emphasizing every word, he read, *"EVER LASTING LIFE!"* Then burying his face in his hands, he whispered, "Oh, thank God!"

The lateness of the hour was forgotten! I was rejoicing with the hosts of Heaven! Another soul had entered in.

May God help me write this in a way that will move your heart in the way it moved mine the night it took place. The Center was closed but two boys remained in the darkness. I am remembering the stillness that came down that night, a stillness that comes only when a soul hangs in the balance. I was standing back in the darkness, listening and crying and praying. Joe, a short little serviceman, a country boy whose ruddy face shines with a holy light, stood in the darkness at our front door, and was lovingly blocking it from the other boy who was desperately under conviction and wanted to get out. I stood in the background and listened. Joe, crying out with the tenderest pleadings was saying, "Oh, please don't go out without Jesus! He died for you! Don't go! Oh, please don't go out without Jesus. . ." but the door opened and a boy went out into the night—into the dark night of

72

sin that grows darker and darker as he faces eternal doom—the blackness of darkness forever. Where is he tonight? Will anyone else ever plead for his soul? Is there a little mother somewhere praying for her boy? *"Is it nothing to you, all ye that pass by?"* Millions grieved for our President Kennedy when he died, a few grieved for his soul, but who grieved for the 120,000 other souls who died that same day without Christ? Our Saviour so grieved for them that He left the Ivory Palaces to redeem them. He wept over the multitudes, because they were as sheep, having no Shepherd. May God help us to care and share His burden for the lost. *"They that sow in tears shall reap in joy. He that goeth forth and weepeth, bearing precious seed, shall doubtless come again with rejoicing, bringing his sheaves with him."* Ps. 126:5,6

> *"With a soul blood-bought, and heart aglow—*
> *Redeemed by the Lord and free—*
> *I ask, as I pass down the busy street,*
> *'Is it only the crowd I see?'*
>
> *Do I lift my eyes with a careless gaze*
> *That pierces no deep-down woe?*
> *Have I naught to give to the teeming throng*
> *Of the wealth of the love that I know?*
>
> *Oh, let me look at the throng as my Saviour did,*
> *'Til mine eyes with tears grow dim.*
> *Let me look 'til I pity the wandering ones,*
> *And love them and win them for Him."*

OUR PRAYER ROOM

It seems to me that this book would not be complete without a special article about our prayer room. As I have tried to write about this wonderful place, I have keenly sensed how feeble my efforts are. I can only pray that as you read, the blessed Holy Spirit will reveal to your heart, that which I could never put into mere words.

Not just another room, —but a holy place.

A place that words could never adequately describe, —the holy of holies.

A place made sacred by the penitent tears and prayers of thousands of our servicemen who have knelt here and had their lives changed by a mighty miracle of God's grace.

Yes, a place, God's place, —the most important place in the Center. Here God fulfills the purposes of all our prayers, gifts and labors.

Here in this place, angels hover low as eternal decisions are recorded in Heaven.

In this place repentant tears have flowed until they formed puddles on the floor.

In this place a multitude of sins have been cleansed in the precious blood of Jesus.

In this place the joy of the Lord began for thousands, as the burdens and guilt of sins were lifted.

To pause and meditate on this sacred place draws the tears of adoration for our great God of mercy, who makes

Himself known at this mercy seat, and fills the soul with His glory.

"Come ye disconsolate, where'er ye languish;
Come to the mercy-seat, fervently kneel;
Here bring your wounded hearts, here tell your anguish;
Earth has no sorrow that Heaven cannot heal.

Joy of the desolate, light of the straying,
Hope of the penitent, fadeless and pure,
Here speaks the Comforter, tenderly saying,
'Earth has no sorrow that Heaven cannot cure.'

Here see the bread of life; see waters flowing
Forth from the throne of God, pure from above;
Come to the feast of love; come, ever knowing
Earth has no sorrow but Heaven can remove."

After renting the Center building for many years, God answered prayer and opened the door for us to purchase a permanent Center home. When we moved we left behind many sacred memories. —The little prayer room where so many had wept their way to Jesus. —There was probably not an inch of floor space in the Center where I had not stood and pled with sinners to come to Christ. —So, when we walked out and turned the key in the door for the last time, there was a tinge of sorrow. That night the Lord brought a wonderful promise to me, *"The glory of this latter house shall be greater than of the former, saith the Lord of hosts."* Haggai 2:9

That year we were holding our Annual Bible and Missionary Conference in the new Center. We did most of the work ourselves and all of us, including friends and board-members, were almost exhausted trying to get it finished for this wonderful occasion. There was still so much to do. It was the night preceding the Conference before I was able to finish the most important place in the Center, —the prayer room. It was with thankfulness that I worked and each task was done lovingly and prayerfully. From the beginning, when I padded the prayer bench, to the last finishing touch of placing the Bible upon it, God was speaking to my heart. As I finished and stood in the doorway surveying this sacred, 'Holy of Holies', the Lord's nearness almost overwhelmed me and a deep yearning to be alone with Him filled my whole being as the Lord bid me tarry awhile. —But I reminded myself that I shouldn't take the time. —A multitude of tasks awaited me. —Everyone else was working so hard. —It was already so late and I was so weary. Yet the tug of God was so compelling that I had to close the door and fall on my knees before Him. His glory filled that little room and hovered over me in the holy stillness. Once again came the promise of His blessing upon this place. As tears flowed down my face and began to drop, my first impulse was that I must not let them mar the new prayer bench. —But God was speaking to me and it was as if He said, "Dorothy, this is the way it must be. If your tears are not here, there will never be any more. I called you apart because I wanted yours to be the first tears on this, my altar. It is only as you go forth with tears and a broken heart for the souls of men that I can use you. Only then can I bring others, broken and weeping to this place." *"They that sow in tears shall reap in joy. He that goeth forth and weepeth, bearing precious seed shall doubtless come again with rejoicing, bringing his sheaves with him."*. . . . . .

> *"Sweet hour of prayer, sweet hour of prayer,*
> *That calls me from a world of care,*
> *And bids me at my Father's throne*
> *Make all my wants and wishes known . . ."*

One lad, coming from our little prayer room, shifted his weight from one foot to the other, then moved his shoulders this way and that and turning to us exclaimed, "You know, I believe I lost weight in there!" Yes, thank God, burdens are lifted at Calvary! *"The blood of Jesus Christ, God's Son, cleanseth us from ALL sin."*

One day one of our Christian boys walked into the Center, exchanged greetings with one of the workers, and then asked, "Where's Dorothy?"

The worker replied, "She is in the prayer room with a young man." Then she smiled and said, "I think another BABE IS BEING BORN INTO THE LORD'S FAMILY."

A broad grin crept across the Christian boy's face and he said, "MY, isn't that a wonderful little ETERNITY WARD!"

Yes, we thank God for that little "ETERNITY WARD" where many precious babes are born into the Lord's family.

> "There's a spot that will ever be sacred to me,
> While the years of earth's pilgrimage roll,
> In His beauty 'tis vivid in my memory,
> Where Jesus came into my soul.
>
> I'll cherish the spot where Jesus saved me
> Where to Him I yielded control.
> Could I go there today—
> I would kneel down and pray
> Where Jesus came into my soul.
>
> I was sick, I was wandering, unable to see
> 'Til I gave the dear Saviour control,
> Then the gates to His sheepfold
> Swung open for me,
> And Jesus spoke peace to my soul.
>
> With my Lord I am safe in the fold of His grace
> And I'm happy wher'er I may be
> Still I cherish with reverence that first altar place
> Where my Saviour, from sin set me free."

THE SALT OF THE EARTH

"Ye are the salt of the earth; but if the salt have lost his savour, wherewith shall it be salted? it is thenceforth good for nothing, but to be cast out, and to be trodden under foot of men." —Matt. 5:13

"Salt is good: but if the salt have lost his savour, wherewith shall it be seasoned? It is neither fit for the land, nor yet for the dunghill; but men cast it out. He that hath ears to hear, let him hear." —Luke 14:34, 35

This morning I received a long-distance telephone call from my sister. She had some questions about this verse and we had quite a lengthy discussion. God spoke to my heart. Jesus says here that if we will not witness to sinners that we might save them from Hell, we are good for neither God, man nor the dunghill. ——good for nothing!

These words from Jesus are drastic, but how few Christians heed them. Just look around today and you will find very few witnessing Christians. Mankind is floundering in ignorance and wickedness, ready to putrefy. Why? *"—the salt hath lost its savour."* It is appalling, but day after day in the Center we hear these words after we witness to a boy, "No one ever told me how to be saved before." In fact, the three last souls I had for Jesus said just that.

Two boys sat at the desk talking together about what a nice place the Center was. To a question as to who provided it, one boy stated, "Christian Science." Rather shocked, I inquired as to where he got his false information to make such a statement. As if caught, they both walked back to the

counter saying, "It isn't? Well, what religion is this then?"
My Bible was handy so I pushed it closer and explained that
we were real Christians and took our authority from one
Book alone, God's Holy Word. We talked on about Jesus and
often they made comments such as, "It's so good to talk to
someone like you . . . You know that Bible from cover to cover
don't you? . . . I'm a member of a Church but I see that I'm not
saved . . . I've never had the privilege of an experience such
as you had with Jesus." To this last comment, I said, "As a
Christian, speaking for Jesus, I would like to extend this
privilege to you boys. —Will you kneel with me and accept
my Saviour for your very own. . . ?" They hesitated and I
continued to carefully choose verses, praying in my heart
that God would give me the right ones in this crucial time as
these two very precious souls hung in the balance. I quoted
Revelation 3:20: *"Behold, I stand at the door, and knock: if
any man hear my voice, and open the door, I will come into
him, and will sup with him, and he with me."* Just as it has
countless times before, the tug of this Scripture broke down
their last wall of resistance and both boys accepted Christ as
their Saviour. Oh, the thrill of leading them to the prayer
room and then to Jesus . . . Then to hear these words, "You
are the only one who ever took time to tell me about Jesus.
How can we ever thank you!"

Stewart was reading a Bible and as we visited he told me
he had taken a year of Seminary and was planning to be a
preacher. He admitted he was not sure of Heaven and didn't
know what being "born again" meant. Satan had deceived
him with many false ideas such as, "Sin is not sin if the
person involved has a good motive, etc. . ." When all these
crumbled in the light of God's Word, he was honorable
enough to admit his error and sat back and listened as I took
my Bible and explained how a man can be born again by the
Spirit of God by receiving Jesus as Saviour. When I asked for
his decision, he answered in a straightforward way, "Yes, I
certainly will. I believe this is what I have been searching
for. No one ever told me the things you did today. Even in

Seminary, no one ever told me that I needed to be saved, not even my professors." What if I had failed this precious soul?

Lest some should think the Center is the only place to witness, or that they do not have such opportunities, I would like to share several experiences which I had this week to speak a word for Christ, —all outside the Center.

At the drug store I was looking for a Popular Mechanics magazine for the Center when a young lady came over and began cutting and unwrapping a stack of magazines about three feet high. "This is our best seller," she said. I glanced up and saw "PLAYBOY MAGAZINE" and the young lady sweetly smiling at me for my comment. I tried to be kind but honest as I said, "It shouldn't even be sold at all. It is filthy and I am sure that if you were a Christian you would not want to have a part in putting such an obscene magazine into the hands of our young people." Her face turned crimson and she tried desperately to defend it in every way, and ended by saying, "They say it has lots of good articles in it, too." I reminded her that this was the Devil's tactic to mix a little good with his filth. —He is the great deceiver and he deceives many just this way. Then I told her of boys who often brought this filthy magazine into the Center and as I talked to them about Jesus, how they did all kinds of things trying to hide even the cover from me, but when they accept Christ, the Lord gives them a love for a Holy Book, the Bible, and the filth goes into the wastebasket. There was a holy stillness in the whole store as this girl and the manager listened while I warned her of the coming judgment and presented the gospel to her. With such a God-given opening, how could I have failed them and Jesus?

Yesterday I made a hurried trip to the dime store and as the clerk waited on me, the din and beat of the store's "jungle music" was difficult for me to endure. As I waited, I made a few remarks expressing my dislike for it and as a Christian I would appreciate hearing a hymn sometime when I came in. (How are they to know if we don't express our wishes?) I continued by saying, "I believe you have enough Christians who patronize your store and who love the old gospel hymns, to merit your playing one, at least once in awhile." As I gave a few more words of testimony for Jesus, I noticed that the Lord had the store's manager near-by and he was listening too. Nervously he tried to write on a pad in his hand and then made a hasty retreat. The young lady thanked me for my words and her warmness told me that I had gained a friend who respected my Christian testimony. What if I had been too ashamed of Jesus to speak these words for Him to needy souls? —Jesus says I would be *"good for nothing!"*

As I rode home in a cab a few nights ago, the driver was dreading the late hours when he would have to haul all the "drunks" back to the base. God was giving me another opening to tell a soul about Jesus and His power to deliver from every bondage, including drink. The driver listened and was reminded of his father, with Jesus now, but who had been a faithful gospel preacher. The cab driver did not accept Christ, but when I left he refused to accept my fare, asking rather that I pray for him. God would not have wanted me to have failed this precious soul.

One day I walked to the grocery store. Carrying two large sacks of groceries, I was almost to the Center when I noticed a young serviceman, about eighteen years old, drunk and leaning on a lamp post outside a tavern. —He was some mother's son and I was moved with compassion for him. I paused, put down my load, took a gospel tract from my purse and stuffed it into his shirt pocket. As I did this, I said, "Son, this will tell you about Jesus. When you feel better, read it. Jesus loves you and died to save you. He will cleanse your heart from sin and give you victory over sin...." I walked on, but as I crossed the street I heard the shuffling of feet behind me. It was the drunk young man. As he stumbled toward me, he was pleading, "Tell me how! Tell me how!...." Can we deny that the words of Jesus are true when He said, *"Say not ye, There are yet four months, and then cometh harvest? behold, I say unto you, Lift up your eyes, and look on the fields; for they are white already to harvest"* (John 4:35). Again He said, *". . . . The harvest truly is plenteous, but the labourers are few;"* (Matt. 9:37). There is a harvest out there!

Dear Christian friend, what about you and your witness for your Lord? Can Jesus say of you that *"ye are the salt of the earth?"* Are you a witnessing Christian —in the office to your co-workers, —in the school to your teachers and classmates, —in the home to your children, neighbors, that salesman who calls, to your grocer, that store clerk . . . . ."

If these have not heard the story of Jesus from your lips, tell God that you don't want to grieve Him any longer by being *"good for nothing."* Why not start today!

"A missionary is one who never becomes accustomed to the tramp of Christless feet on their way to a lost eternity."

GOOD-BYES

". . . he kneeled down, and prayed with them all. And they all wept sore, . . . Sorrowing most of all for the words which he spake, that they should see his face no more . . ."
—*Acts 20:36-38*

Good-byes! How many thousands of them I have heard! Just when we have learned to know and love a boy, we eventually hear the familiar words, "I'm shipping out next Tuesday for Maine . . . Florida . . . Germany . . . Korea . . . or England . . . ," etc. I can never get used to those good-byes and my heart is always moved. I would like to share some recent ones with you.

It was so easy to love Larrie, with his red hair, shy but sweet smile, and a heart that was so responsive to the voice of God. The first time we witnessed to him, he realized his lost condition, bowed his knee and lifted his heart to Jesus. Our love for him grew as we fellowshipped, studied the Bible and prayed together. It was always a joy to have Larrie for a meal because he enjoyed it so and let us know how much he appreciated it, —But Sunday was the last one and after a little Bible Study we had to say good-bye. Words did not come easy and a lump came into my throat as I watched Larrie sadly turn and walk out the door for the last time. Later, tucked under an article on the counter, we found his little "farewell note" that he had been too bashful to hand us. It said:

"Servicemen's Center? —a home away from home.
This is what this Servicemen's Center means to me.
It is a place where I could go, talk, listen or just be

83

alone. I was saved at this Center, led in the ways of God, and you helped me to find the true path to eternal life. I wish to thank you people from the deepest recesses of my heart. To you people I owe a lot, because my soul was on the way to Hell, but you helped save my soul and changed my life by showing me the way to Heaven. So to the people connected to the Center, I thank you and I pray that others may find what I found, —the Lord Jesus. So once again, thank you all.   Sincerely, Larrie."

So, good-bye Larrie, but I will see you again when Jesus comes for His own!

"My parents wouldn't understand if they knew how I feel tonight. I'm going home, but my heart is so heavy...." Jim was sobbing as he spoke to me. It was his last night at the Center before he shipped out and he sat at the kitchen table with his head in his hands, tears rolling down his cheeks. The Lord has done great things for Jim. We had seen him change from a carnal Christian to one that beamed for God with a burning desire to see souls saved. When he first came into the Center he told us he was saved but we did not see any evidence of the Christ-life. One day I turned to him and said, "Jim, are you satisfied with your life for the Lord?" He replied, "No, I'm not." We showed him from the Word of God how the Lord wants us to present our bodies as a living sacrifice to Him. Our Lord needed young men who would say, "Here I am Lord, use me." The Holy Spirit was striving with his heart and at last he said, "He can have me." Tears began to flow. Jim came to the Lord and surrendered his life. In the following days we marveled at the change in his life that could only be explained by the power of God. He spoke to groups of his buddies with tears of compassion. He passed out thousands of tracts on base and in town. He gave messages in Bible Classes and Young People's Classes that gripped hearts. Many times he worked for hours going from barracks to barracks, inviting the airmen to the Center and to Church. Often he labored long into the night. In Jim we have seen what God can do with a surrendered life, —and so it was with broken hearts and tears that we, too, said good-bye to him as he shipped out, but we rejoice in the fact that we know wherever Jim goes he will be God's man in God's place. With this introduction you will enjoy Jim's own testimony:

"I came to Chanute Field in January to attend Aircraft and Engine Mechanic School. The school was fine, but the weather was terrible, especially for a fellow who came from the land of sunshine (Florida) in one hop. I practically hibernated until along in April. After I finally ventured off the post, one day I happened to drop in at the Christian Service Center. Praise the Lord for that day, because I had a long heart to heart talk with the young lady in charge. I had accepted the Lord Jesus as my personal Saviour in the jungles of darkest New Guinea, but I was not living a Christian life. I was smoking, going to movies and other places of the world. I had never even thought of telling others about the Lord Jesus. That day I saw my awful sin and we knelt in prayer as I asked Him to forgive me and I surrendered my life to Him.

I praise Him for all He has done for me. He has taken away my smoking and other sins and in their place He has given me a burden for souls. I am enjoying a great blessing witnessing to the lost. Last Tuesday at our Soul-winner's Class at the Center, we had a wonderful time with twenty-nine present. I was so happy when two of my buddies accepted the Lord. I shall never forget the Center here, nor what God has done for me through it. I can truly say that they are doing a magnificent job of leading others to Him and helping those who know Him, to live better for Him. Lord willing, I will be returning to my home base in Florida soon. I know I will miss the wonderful fellowship and spiritual help I have found here, but my earnest prayer is that the

Lord will use me for the glory of His kingdom wherever I am. Each of you who read this, please pray for me. May God's blessings abide with you always." —Sgt. James H.

Good-bye, Jim, —but we will meet again around Jesus' throne.

Gary was a Christian boy who found a place to pray and sweet Christian fellowship in the Center... a haven from the sin in his barracks. The day came when he, too, had to tell us good-bye. For over two hours he stood at the door, reluctant to make the break and leave. At last, slipping his hand into his jacket pocket he brought out a prayer cookie, and with a choking voice said to me, "I just had to take one with me... to remember... You know?" —Yes, I know. Gary isn't the first boy I've seen leave with one of those special cookies. Slowly he walked down the street, turned and took one last look at the Center and then walked out of sight. Good-bye for a little time Gary, but we will meet again in Heaven!

Roger, with his rosy cheeks, was one of sterling character, so faithful and dependable. The longer we knew him the more we loved him. He shipped out to Korea, then here and there over the country, but he never forgot the Center. Faithfully every month a letter came, addressed in his familiar handwriting with ten dollars to "help reach other buddies for Jesus." Then one day the phone rang and his father told us that Roger had gone to be with the Lord. On my desk I picked up a letter addressed to us in Roger's hand and I thought, "He was faithful unto the end." —I will never receive another letter and gift from Roger. It is good-bye for a time, but we sorrow not as those who have no hope. At the resurrection we will see Roger again.

One Sunday afternoon God gave us an opportunity to speak to another soul about his need of Jesus. This was a "good" man, respected and close to me, but unsaved. He knew he wasn't saved and needed Jesus, but somehow he would not make a decision. Trembling and with head bowed, he listened in silence for several hours as we gently pleaded with him to come to the Saviour. Oh, how we hated to leave him so desperately under conviction. "—Almost persuaded . . . almost, but lost!" The days slipped by and one night a telephone call came. A chill of horror gripped me as I heard the almost unbelievable word, "Dead." The things of earth never satisfy and this wretched soul had snuffed out his own life. Reason told me that this man could never do this, —but he did. How alone, despondent, and desperate he must have been—without hope and without God. This was an eternal good-bye and my heart has been heavy with sorrow. I cannot bring him back and plead with him, but I can go to those who are still living with the wonderful message of God's redeeming grace. Dear friends, life is empty and useless without Jesus. Souls are lost and desperate, and passing out into eternity one by one. When we meet one who knows not our Christ, do we serve Jesus by talking about HIM, —or do we serve Satan by talking only about "things?" Today, and the few todays we may have left, let us serve our Lord by giving forth His glorious life-giving message to the stranger, the friend, the neighbor, the relative, who come our way.

"... *choose you this day whom YE will serve; ... but as for me and my house, we will serve the Lord.*"   Me too, Joshua.

You talk about your business,
  Your bonds and stocks and gold,
And in all worldly matters
  You are so brave and bold.
But why are you so silent
  About salvation's plan?
Why don't you speak for Jesus,
  And speak out like a man?

You talk about the weather,
  And the crops of corn and wheat,
You speak of friends and neighbors
  That pass along the street;
You call yourself a Christian,
  And like the Gospel plan—

Then why not speak for Jesus,
    And speak out like a man?

Are you ashamed of Jesus
    And the story of the cross,
That you lower His pure banner
    And let it suffer loss?
Have you forgot His suffering?
    Did He die for you in vain?
If not, then live and speak for Jesus
    And speak out like a man!

MY FATHER

"My Jesus I love Thee, I know Thou art mine!
For Thee all the folly of sin I resign—
My gracious Redeemer, my Saviour art Thou—
If ever I loved Thee, my Jesus 'tis now."

Tonight I write this with a heavy but very grateful heart. Only a few days ago I looked down into my dear father's coffin. Tears flowed, but inwardly a deep gratitude and love to the Lord welled up in my heart as over and over again I said, "Thank you Lord Jesus for saving his soul!"

Some time ago I was asked, "Dorothy, in all of your years of serving Jesus, do you have one experience that was especially precious to you?" With little hesitation, I answered, "Yes, when I led my father to Christ." In this Bulletin I have shared many experiences with you, but I have never shared this one. For our Lord's honor and glory, may I do it tonight?

It began back, February 2, 1943, the night I knelt in prayer and received the Lord Jesus as my own personal Saviour. Joy and peace flooded my soul, yet while still on my knees my heart was burdened for my father, mother, brothers and sisters. I knew they were unsaved. That night, before I slept, I wrote a thirty page letter home, pleading with them, as best I could, to come to Jesus for salvation. I spent much time in prayer for them and when I went home on weekends I did my best to make the way to Heaven plain. Often I would go to the barn and help dad with the milking so I could talk to him alone about Jesus. My father was a rather timid reserved person. He listened but made little or no response.

89

As the days passed I grew in the Lord and quite naturally my burden for souls became heavier. My family, not understanding my concern, nor the great change that had taken place in my life, seemed to withdraw from me as I witnessed to them. The more I pled with them to be saved, the more hostile they seemed to become toward me and God's wonderful message of salvation. Often tears flowed because I longed for the love and warmth of my family. Sometimes I felt as if I could not speak to them about Jesus anymore, *". . . but His Word was in mine heart as a burning fire shut up in my bones, and I was weary with forbearing, and I could not stay."* Oh, how I thank God He kept me faithful!

Using all means to reach my loved ones for Christ, I had the Crocketts visit my parents one Sunday afternoon. Brother Crockett spoke to dad, but again my father made little response. That night as I came to Church, Brother Crockett greeted me and then said, "Dorothy, I don't believe your father is saved." I knew this but the Lord used those words to burden my heart. As the service began, the congregation began to sing that great old hymn, *"Jesus is coming to earth again. What if it were today. . . . ?"* I began to sob, saying, "Lord, I don't want you to come today because dad isn't saved . . ." In a strange wonderful way God moved upon my heart. All through the service I wept for my father. Later I sobbed as I walked the mile or so to my room and then, on my knees, I sobbed and prayed all night, asking the Lord to save my dad. Knowing I would have to report for work on Monday and not get home for a week to speak to dad again, I prayed, "Lord, if You want me to go home before next weekend, You make it possible." The next morning I was told I could have the day off. I knew God had arranged this. . . .I feared to go home. . . but I knew I must.

When I got off the bus, I called my folk and father drove into town for me. He expressed his surprise, wondering why I was home on Monday morning. I burst into tears and couldn't talk so my father pulled the car into the side of the road. Between sobs, I said, "Dad, I just can't live any longer if you are not saved." He put his arm around me and said, "Don't cry like that... When we get home we will talk." This was not like dad. When we got home he followed me into the house and we sat down together, dad waiting in silence for me to speak. I was only a baby Christian myself, but the Lord guided me to the right Scripture to make the way to Heaven plain to dad. My father was known as a good, clean-living man, highly respected in the community and had thought this was the way to Heaven. That day, from God's Word, he realized he, too, was a lost, hell-bound sinner and must make that all-important decision and receive Jesus as his own personal Saviour. Together we knelt in God's presence and dad confessed his sin, calling upon the Lord Jesus to come into his heart and save his soul. Almost breathless and overcome with joy, I shall never forget the way dad reached over and took my hand in his as we still knelt before God. Afterward, I asked the Lord to give me a portion of Scripture to read to my father, and in trembling hands my Bible opened to I Peter 1. As I read, it was as if the Lord had just written this wonderful portion for this momentous occasion! Read it. I have since memorized it. *"Blessed be the God and Father of our Lord Jesus Christ, which according to his abundant mercy hath begotten us again unto a lively hope by the resurrection of Jesus Christ from the dead, To an inheritance incorruptible, and undefiled, and that fadeth not away, reserved in heaven for you, Who are kept by the power of God through faith unto salvation ready to be revealed in the last time. Wherein ye greatly rejoice, though now for a season, if need be, ye are in heaviness through manifold temptations: That the trial of your faith, being much more precious than of gold that perisheth, though it be tried with fire, might be found unto praise and honour and glory at the appearing of Jesus Christ:"* (I Peter 1:3-7). Tonight my father is enjoying that *"inheritance incorruptible, and undefiled, and that fadeth not away,"* which was reserved in Heaven for him that day when he came to Christ.

It seemed only fitting and proper that Brother Crockett read this same wonderful portion of Scripture at my father's funeral. What a comfort and joy it brought to our hearts, knowing that although our earthly family circle was broken, it had begun to form in Heaven. Dad is with Jesus.

Tonight I love the Lord with a new and deeper love, and with it has come a greater love and burden for those yet lost and without the Saviour. God tells us that the soul of man is priceless, and then He says, *"He that winneth souls is WISE."* God help us to "walk, not as FOOLS, but as WISE, redeeming the time . . ." Today if death should suddenly come, without warning, to some of your loved ones, as it did to my dad, are any outside the fold? Of all things, life is the frailest. —The unsaved soul hangs by a slender thread over the flames of eternal Hell, —a thread that can be singed asunder at any moment. Do we REALLY care? God help us to fall on our faces before Him and stay there until our hearts are broken for the lost. Then *"go quickly"* to that father- mother - wife - husband - brother - sister - son - daughter - neighbor - or friend with the message of salvation. TODAY! Tomorrow may be too late!

"They that sow in tears shall reap in joy. He that goeth forth and weepeth, bearing precious seed, shall doubtless come again with rejoicing, bringing his sheaves with him."
—Psalm 126:5, 6

"They that be WISE shall shine as the brightness of the firmament; and they that turn many to righteousness as the stars for ever and ever." *—Dan. 12:3*

CHRISTIAN, DO YOU WANT TO BE A SOUL-WINNER?

If you want to be a soul-winner you can be, because God has already called you and wants to use you to reach the lost. Jesus said, *". . . Follow Me, and I will make you fishers of men."* —Matt. 4:19

Jesus also said, *". . . . If any man will come after Me, let him deny himself, and take up his cross and follow Me"* (Matt. 16:24). It is never easy to serve Jesus. He calls for a disciplined life. God has no short-cuts to spirituality. Give yourself to prayer and the study of His holy Word. Memorize it. (If we don't care enough to diligently study and memorize the Word, I don't believe God can ever use us.)

I believe the memorization of God's Word was one of the greatest things God used in my life to make me a soul-winner. Below are some of the Scriptures I have memorized and use in soul-winning. Look them up. Underline them in your Bible. Pray and ask God to help you memorize them. Remember, people are saved by hearing the Word of God. *". . . faith cometh by hearing, and hearing by the Word of God."* —Romans 10:17

SCRIPTURES TO LEAD SOULS TO CHRIST

1. **All Are Sinners and Condemned**

    Romans 3:23
    Isa. 53:6
    Jer. 17:9
    Ecc. 7:20
    James 2:10
    Romans 6:23   Isa. 59:2
    Ezek. 18:20   Romans 5:12
    Romans 3:10-20   Isa. 64:6

2. Jesus Died For Sinners

   John 3:16
   Romans 5:8
   I Peter 2:24
   I Peter 3:18
   Isa. 53:5
   Isa. 53:12

3. We Cannot Save Ourselves

   Eph. 2:8,9
   Titus 3:5   Jas. 2:10
   Romans 6:23   Isa. 64:6
   Gal. 2:16   II Cor. 5:21
   Prov. 14:12

4. Only Jesus Can Save

   Acts 4:12
   John 14:6   I John 1:7
   John 8:24   Romans 10:9,10,13
   John 8:32,36   Isa. 1:18
   Hebrews 7:25   Acts 3:19
   John 3:3,6,7   James 4:14
   John 1:12,13   Matt. 16:26
   I Pet. 1:18,19   Heb. 9:27

5. Invitation of Jesus

   Isa. 55:6
   Isa. 1:18
   Acts 3:19
   Rev. 3:20
   II Cor. 6:2
   Joshua 24:15

"For the Word of God is quick, and powerful, and sharper than any twoedged sword, piercing even to the dividing asunder of soul and spirit, and of the joints and marrow, and is a discerner of the thoughts and intents of the heart."
                                             —Hebrews 4:12

ARE YOU SAVED AND SURE OF HEAVEN?

THE BIBLE SAYS. . . .

> that you are either saved or lost. There is no in between. *"He that hath the Son hath life, and he that hath not the Son of God hath not life."*
>
> I John 5:12

THE BIBLE SAYS. . . .

> that Christ came to this sin cursed world to seek and to save that which was lost.   Luke 19:10

THE BIBLE SAYS. . . .

> that you CAN be saved. *"That if thou shalt confess with thy mouth the Lord Jesus, and shalt believe in thine heart that God hath raised Him from the dead, thou shalt be saved."*
>
> Romans 10: 9

> *"Verily, verily, I say unto you, He that heareth my word, and believeth on him that sent me, hath everlasting life, and shall not come into condemnation; but is passed from death unto life."*
>
> John 5:24

THE BIBLE SAYS. . . .

> that tomorrow may be too late. *"Boast not thyself of tomorrow; for thou knowest not what a day may bring forth."*   Prov. 27:1

"Behold, now is the accepted time; behold, now is the day of salvation."

II Cor. 6:2

JESUS SAYS. . . .

"Behold, I stand at the door and knock; if any man hear my voice, and open the door, I will come in to him, and will sup with him, and he with me."

Rev. 3:20

If you sincerely want to be saved and begin a new life with Jesus, make this your prayer:

"Lord Jesus, I know I am a sinner and deserve Hell, but I believe You loved me and died on the cross, shedding your blood to save me. Just now I receive You as my own personal Saviour. Come into my heart, wash away all my sins in your precious blood and save my soul today. Thank you Lord Jesus for loving me and dying for me. Teach me to love You and live for You.   Amen."

_____
name

_____
date

After praying and accepting Christ as your Saviour, I suggest that you sign your name and the date. Also jot it down in your Bible. It will be a reminder of the moment when you accepted Jesus as your Saviour, and thereby received God's wonderful gift of eternal life. John 10:27-29

If you need more help, please feel free to write me. I care and want to help you make sure of Heaven.

Dorothy Myers
% Christian Service Center
113 Sangamon Ave.
Rantoul, Ill. 61866

—LIFT UP YOUR EYES AND LOOK ON THE FIELDS—

Over 2,000,000 young men are in the service of our country. This is a vast mission field, white unto harvest. Our SERVICE CENTERS are "LIGHT-HOUSES" beaming forth the gospel message of God's redeeming grace.

Thousands of servicemen come from other countries to America for training. Many of these are saved in our Centers and return to their own country, taking the gospel to their people. ——MISSIONS ——HOME AND ABROAD

—YOUR GIFTS AND PRAYERS HELP US REACH THESE FOR JESUS—

If you would like to receive our monthly publication, "The Good News Bulletin", please write to any of the Centers listed below.

CHRISTIAN SERVICE CENTERS

113 Sangamon Ave
Rantoul, IL 61866

319 C. Street
Lawton, OK 73501

Crockett & Broadway
San Antonio, TX 78298

8410 Hampton Blvd.
Norfolk, VA 23505